an ANGEL
in the FLAME

a tale of two saviors

AN ANGEL
IN THE FLAME

a tale of two saviors

C. GENE WILKES

LEAFWOOD
PUBLISHERS
Abilene, TX

AN ANGEL IN THE FLAME
A Tale of Two Saviors

Copyright 2008 by C. Gene Wilkes

ISBN 978-0-89112-558-7

Printed in the United States of America

Cover design by Greg Jackson, Thinkpen Design
Interior text design by Sandy Armstrong

For information contact:
Leafwood Publishers, Abilene, Texas
1-877-816-4455 toll free
www.leafwoodpublishers.com

08 09 10 11 12 13 14 / 7 6 5 4 3 2 1

"As the flame blazed up from the altar toward heaven, the angel of the Lord ascended in the flame."

—JUDGES 13:20

TABLE OF CONTENTS

ACKNOWLEDGEMENTS

No writer writes alone, and the writing of this book is no exception. I want to thank Lynn Anderson for his years of friendship, mentoring, and belief in me as a leader and writer. He invested his time and influence to make this manuscript available to Leafwood Publishers. His ministry in my life and the lives of others is a model I want to emulate.

I want to thank Leonard Allen of Leafwood for his personal attention and care in the process of editing and producing this book. I am forever grateful for the opportunity to help people trust Jesus through the publishing ministry he leads. Editors make writers better in every way, and I must acknowledge my gratitude to Heidi Nobles for her careful attention to details and inquiries to keep my writing clear and focused.

I must thank the people who are Legacy Church and the Leadership Team who encourage me and give me the time to put my calling into writing. Their love and appreciation energize me and give me the confidence to share with the reader what I share with them. They have been kind to allow my ministry to grow in so many ways through the twenty-plus years of ministry together.

My wife, Kim, is my best friend and encourager. She has sacrificed time together in order for me to write, and I am grateful to her in so many ways. I pray where I am more like Samson I will become more like Jesus for her.

C. Gene Wilkes
Ash Wednesday, 2008

Introduction

This is a tale of two saviors. Two men whom God chose to rescue his people. Two men anyone familiar with history would call heroes among their people. Two men who represent the best and worst the human experience have to offer. One was the Gladiator and the Hulk wrapped into one. The other was a humble carpenter who led no army or held no office, yet in his death caused a cosmic ripple that vibrates through our universe today. The first is a type of the latter, and the latter the fulfillment of the first. Both are part of God's story to capture the hearts of men and women with his love, but only one lived out God's ultimate purpose for his life. This tale is about Samson and Jesus.

Samson had the strength of Hercules and the vanity of Narcissus. Yet he was not an ancient mythical figure. He was part of God's history with Israel. His life, exploits, and seduction by Delilah have fascinated writers, poets, artists, and filmmakers through the ages. He is one of the best-known Old Testament characters even among those who did not grow up attending Sunday school. Samson is every man's dream of physical strength and every woman's vision of male beauty. He was the Arnold Schwarzenegger of his day—strongman turned political figure. And, if they had films then, he would have starred in them like his twentieth-century counterpart. Samson still draws attention to himself because he causes us to ask questions like, "How could someone so blessed mess up so badly?" or, "Why did God continue to depend on a guy who only used God for his purposes? I thought pious people were the only ones God used?" or, "What would have happened if he had done everything God told him to do? What would history look like then?" And, on a less philosophical level, we all want to know what Samson and Delilah looked like and whom their children would have turned out to be.

Samson is an enigma among the saints who spot the pages of Scripture. God announced his birth to a barren woman, laid out his life plan, and empowered him with the Lord's Spirit to perform magnificent feats of strength and agility. Yet his life ended far from God in the hands of his enemies. He died and lived alone. His handsome hair was both the source of his strength and his downfall. His life counted as one who held off his country's enemies for twenty years, but on the whole, Samson's story stings like an open sore of squandered opportunity.

As we watch Samson's life, we may find it difficult to overlook parallels to the life of Jesus. Setting aside Jesus' special place in history as God's only Son, Samson and Jesus were both leaders sent by God to deliver Israel and his offspring. Angels announced their births. Both were first born sons who defeated the enemies of God. Both died at the hands of others, and their deaths affected many. Both were saviors. But there the similarities end. For in character, these men are as different as creature and Creator, man and God.

In this tale of two saviors, I want to introduce you to Jesus of Nazareth through the backdoor of Samson's life. Samson and Jesus play strategic roles in God's cosmic redemption play, yet Samson is a poor understudy to the main character, Jesus. By coming to Jesus through Samson, you begin to understand why God had to send his Son. With leaders like Samson, the human race clearly needed the Savior, not another hero!

Coming into the house of God through the backdoor of Samson's life allows us to meet a family hero with a spotted past. His picture hangs on a wall along with others who served the purposes of God, but he's not one the family likes to talk about. He was a womanizing warrior whom God used to irritate Israel's enemies, and, in the end, he gave his life for the family, but he could have done so much more. He is a counterpart to his distant cousin, Jesus. His picture could have hung in the hall of heroes with King David and Solomon, but he never gave himself completely to God, so his face hangs in the family room in the corner, next to King Saul's portrait. In that part of the house hang the portraits of the rowdy ones you learn about when you have been in the family long enough for the tribe to trust you with the seedy stories about their heritage.

Meeting Jesus through Samson's life is like entering through the family's backdoor. The Old Testament is the kitchen and dining room of your Father's house. There you meet your family, eat with them, taste their food, and hear their stories. You share hope for the future as your Father reveals his plans for the family. Just through this backdoor, you hear about your crazy uncles and aunts while grownups teach you that although your relatives messed up royally, they are still part of the family—important parts of the family, and you benefit from their walking the earth. At the age-darkened table, you receive the bread of life and learn to trust those who provide it. You find you are a member of a clan of faith that has been around much longer than you can imagine and that you have received all that is good and bad from their decisions. You learn of patriarchs and matriarchs who shaped the flow of family history. You laugh 'til you cry at your family's mishaps and the messes they got themselves into.

At your Father's table you hold hands and pray for each other. You cry for those who suffer among you and for those who have died. You share the grief of those who have gone and the hope of those who have been born since the last time you gathered around the table together. Coming into your Father's house through the backdoor and sitting with others at the table is the best way to know your family.

Hearing the stories of your deceased relatives will help you to see how God can use both his faithful Son, Jesus, and a self-centered son, Samson, to complete God's eternal purposes. You will hear the tale of two saviors, one who lived and died for himself and the other who lived and died for others. God used both to save people's lives—one did it God's way, the other his own way. Samson's story will give you hope that God can use your God-given potential in spite of your selfish use of talent and gifts. Hearing the story of Jesus from Samson's place at the family table will give you hope that God can redeem even our most self-centered choices for eternal purposes.

Come on in. It's okay if the screen door slams behind you. The table's set. Join the family.

Chapter One

Into the Stuff of Life

Do not forget to entertain strangers,
for by so doing some people have entertained angels without knowing it.

—Hebrews 13:2

We meet Samson's parents like we meet new characters in the middle of a play. The story has been going on for some time, and the storyteller introduces us to them as actors walking onto the stage in Act III. The Book of Judges records part of the story of God's purposes to rescue all people back to him. It tells about the time between conquest and kingdom. This period in Israel's life was like America in the days of Lewis and Clark. America was a new nation birthed from revolution and constitution. It was battle-proven and at peace. But while its people gave allegiance to the same flag, they mostly lived as they had always lived: in separate communities trying to survive and carve out a place in the wilderness. The tribes of Israel lived like those early Americans when Samson was born. Joshua had led the twelve tribes of Israel over the Jordan River to overpower the inhabitants of the Promised Land. They had done this by divine mandate and power. Their covenant with God and the promise of new land held their loyalties together. Once they drove out their enemies, they divided the land and began to settle in. At last, the promise of land to Abraham and the Exodus added up to the sum of God's provisions. Israel lived off the "crops they did not plant and drank from wells they did not dig."[1]

The Bible tells us that once the tribes divided up the land of Canaan, they fell into a cyclical pattern of living that became predictable *and* destructive. The storyteller simply described the situation this way: "the sons of Israel did evil in the sight of the Lord."[2] The people of Jehovah began to worship the gods of those who lived around them. If you have trouble understanding these people, you may say, "How could they be so blatantly disrespectful to God?" Let me explain how they came to this place in life.

It may have gone something like this. Let's say Joseph, a member of the Benjamin tribe, moved into a Canaanite neighborhood as part of the conquering people. He built a home and planted some wheat. A Canaanite neighbor gave up some of his farmland to the invaders, but he too planted his fields as he had always done. When harvest time came around, Joseph noticed his neighbor's wheat field yielded more grain than his did. Being the curious neighbor and wanting more from his field, he went to his neighbor's house and asked, "How'd you get more wheat than me?" His neighbor showed him the grain he used and how he kept the weeds out, and he may have also said, "My god, Baal, made it grow."

"Baal?" Joseph asked. This was new information to a worshipper of the Lord.

"Yeah, you know, the god who causes the seasons to come and go and the crops to flourish. I would never plant a crop without honoring Baal," his neighbor said as he picked a head of wheat from his higher-yield field.

"I believe that the God of Israel makes those things happen," Joseph confessed. "If you remember correctly, our God allowed us to whip you guys and take this land."

"You may be right about that. Our people are lousy fighters anyway. Never much cared for fightin' myself. Believe what you want, but the fact is, my fields yield more wheat than yours, and I believe Baal made it happen." Joseph's neighbor confidently smiled at his simple yet profound reasoning. He continued, "And, to show you I have no hard feelings toward you or your god, why don't you come to worship with me at the temple in town. We worship tomorrow. We have interactive worship, and hey, it can't hurt. You want more wheat, don't you?"

Joseph was silent as he considered the faith of his youth and the potential yield of his crops. He knew about the temple prostitutes and his father's warnings about keeping the covenant God had made with Israel—but there were the crops. "What part of 'thou shalt not have other gods before me' don't you understand?" his father would ask. But his father had died in the wilderness. Now, it was time for him to make his own future. After a few moments, he said, "All right, I'll go with you. I guess it's better to have two gods growing your fields than just one."

On that day, Joseph and his Canaanite neighbor struck up a lifelong friendship. It was also the beginning of troubles for the tribes of Israel.

The evil of God's people led to judgment by God through other countries, and the people fell under great distress. Once again, they realized they needed a savior. God responded to his people's cries by raising up "judges," or deliverers. These deliverers in those days were not like a man or woman who sat in a courtroom and ruled on civil and criminal cases: although they seemed to have some judicial powers, most were warrior-judges. These warriors of God, both male and female, were chosen by God to deliver Israel from those who threatened their ability to hold on to the Promised Land. The biblical storyteller writes, "the LORD was with the judge and delivered them [the tribes of Israel] from their enemies all the days of the judge."[3] God's motivation for raising up a judge was to deliver his people. This act was motivated by God's mercy. The writer continues, "for the LORD was moved to pity by their groaning because of those who oppressed and harassed them." Another word for pity here is mercy. Like a loving parent who sees her child responding to her discipline, God was moved by mercy to save those who groaned under the weight of judgment.

Samson was one of these judges whom God raised up to save Israel. Here is how his tale began.

A Visit from an Angel

During this pioneers-turning-into-settlers era of Israel, an angel of the Lord appeared to Samson's mother. This otherworld creature came to tell her she would have a son who would be God's deliverer. We never know the name of Samson's mother. We only know her as "Manoah's wife." What we do know is she was unable to have children. Infertility was more than a personal problem in that day. Children were a family's workforce, its status in the tribe, its 401(k). No children meant no future. Ancient society considered women who could not conceive cursed of God, and the women were often discarded or replaced with those who could bear children.

Infertility still affects the wellbeing of couples who want to be mothers and fathers. Now we have technological alternatives to remedy barrenness. You do not have to go childless if you do not want to—that is, if you have the money to invest in the fertilization process. The poor still go childless, but those with means can pursue technological solutions to fulfill their natural desires.

A drawback to manipulating sperm, egg, and womb is the temptation to put your trust in technology rather than in God. Technology is one of the "little g" gods of our culture. Our first question is too often, "What did the doctor say?" The answer to that question becomes gospel for family and friends—and the church. Just like the Israelites in Canaan who had to choose in whom they would put their trust, so Christ's followers in today's developed countries must choose where their ultimate loyalties lie.

I am not suggesting that those who use technology (as we all do) do not trust God. If that were true, using a computer to write about the things of God would be wrong. My point is that the temptation is to trust technology over the providence and power of God. We would rather change our circumstances than submit to them. We argue that being childless "just can't be God's will for my life," when thousands of children wait, without homes, for parents who will love them. Not having what we want sometimes deepens our faith more than when we have all we need.

Samson's mother, though, did not have our choices to reverse her physical condition, so she lived without a child and with all the insults and insecurities that accompanied her state in life. Into the stuff of life, an angel of the Lord appeared to the nameless, childless woman. She did not know that the "man of God" was an angel at this point in the story. She did know he was more divine than any man she had ever seen.

Throughout the Bible, angels are messengers of God. God created them to worship and to serve him alone, and they bring the message of God to those

God chooses to join him in his purposes. God's voice is deafening to human ears, so an angel muffles the words of God when the Spirit is silent. Whenever an angel appears on the scene you can be certain God has something to tell about what he is doing in creation in order to woo wandering people back to him.

Manoah's wife opened her space to a visitor, a stranger, an alien to her world. She did not know he was an angel. She simply welcomed the one who showed up in the middle of her daily routine. By doing so, she practiced the not-yet-written biblical advice not to "forget to entertain strangers, for by so doing some people have entertained angels without knowing it."[4] She showed kindness to a stranger, and by her actions she made it possible for the angel of God to share the message sent to her from the throne of God. God's message to Samson's mother through this visiting stranger was,

> You are sterile and childless, but you are going to conceive and have a son. Now see to it that you drink no wine or other fermented drink and that you do not eat anything unclean, because you will conceive and give birth to a son. No razor may be used on his head, because the boy is to be a Nazirite, set apart to God from birth, and he will begin the deliverance of Israel from the hands of the Philistines.

God sends angels to tell the truth, not grant one's wishes. They enter human time and space on mission from God.

The message began with "you are sterile and childless." Most people don't like God beginning his messages with what we know is wrong with ourselves. We don't want to talk about our flaws. We want God to overlook our imperfections and only tell us how he will help us. But, God starts with reality before he leads us to new life. Take sin, for example. We want to know we are right with God without hearing we are personally responsible for the sorry state we got ourselves in. We want salvation without the realities of sin and hell, but without them, who needs a savior? Samson's mother quietly listened to the facts about her life, and in doing so, she heard God's plan to let her join in what God would do to save his people.

"But you are going to conceive and have a son" was the promise. "Here's who you are, but here's what God can do through you" was the message.

Hearing the truth about her condition made what God would do even more stunning. "A son . . . set apart to God from birth." Her desert experience was suddenly drenched with a spring shower of hope. She would not only have a son but a son whose life would have divine purpose. I think that, like Hannah who bore Samuel, Samson's mother gladly would have granted God all rights and privileges to her baby even if God had not insisted it be that way from the beginning. Sometimes it is easier to dedicate those things to God that so clearly come from God. It is all the things that seem to come by our efforts that are hard to commit to God. We think they are ours, when all we have is from God.

Children Set Apart

Children conceived after a visit by an angel seem destined to fulfill God's divine plan, and we may find it relatively easy to imagine dedicating these children to God. But what about the "oops" children that show up fifteen years into marriage? What about the unwanted child growing in the womb of a sixteen-year-old? Are these not children who should be "set apart to God from birth"? Don't let the angel's message distort your view of births unannounced by angels. God has divine purposes for those lives, too.

What difference would it make if our children believed about themselves that they had been "set apart to God from birth"? A practice at our church is "dedication of home and family." For the uninitiated it is often confused with christening, but for those in the congregation, it is an opportunity for parents to stand before the church to dedicate their homes to be training schools for godly and moral character. For these dedications, we ask parents to choose a verse to be read as a blessing for their child. I am always moved as I read the promises parents choose for their children. "'For I know the plans I have for you,' declares the LORD, 'plans to prosper you and not to harm you . . . Before I formed you in the womb I knew you, before you were born I set you apart.'" I wonder when those children will read his or her parents' blessings, when the words will come to mean to them what it meant to their parents, who sought to bless their newborns.

"Go be you" is what I tell my girls when we part. That means, "Go be the woman God has created you to become." They know that their parents are convinced that they are no mistake or accident but here because God has a purpose for their lives. If they will simply go be who God has made them to be, they can find all their hearts long for. Parents do not need to read a Dr. Phil book to instill confidence in their children. If we help our children to believe God made them and has a purpose for their lives, then like Samson, they will have the potential to live lives that make eternal differences.

AN AWESOME ANGEL OF GOD

Samson's mother spoke matter-of-factly about the angel's visit to her husband, saying, "A man of God came to me. He looked like an angel of God, very awesome. I didn't ask where he came from, and he didn't tell me his name." All she knew was the man looked like *an angel of God* would look like if she did see one, *very awesome*. She didn't need to know where he came from so she didn't ask—and quite possibly, he wouldn't have told her if she did.

The Bible describes angels as huge beings in Genesis[5] and flying, six-winged ones in Isaiah.[6] Some are majestic creatures that move from eternal dimensions to enter ours. Sometimes people know them for who they are. Sometimes they don't. Sarah didn't recognize as messengers of God the men who made her laugh when she overheard them telling Abraham she would have a child at ninety years of age,[7] but Daniel, the prophet, fell on his face when Gabriel appeared to explain a vision to him,[8] and Samson's mother called her visitor "awesome."

We have trouble experiencing anything awesome today. I believe that is why "extreme" this or that has caught the heart of postmoderns. In centuries past, nature called the hearts of people to the divine. Since we have moved our lives inside, away from sunsets, mountain vistas, and valleys divided by streams, we must push to the edge of common experiences to get a sense of the majesty that creation alone once brought us. We have so shrunk our world into PDAs and wireless phones connected to the Internet that few things wow us anymore. It becomes harder to bring wonder to a life incubated in front of computer-generated disaster movies, X-boxes, and handheld computers.

It took J. K. Rowling's Harry Potter to bring wonder to a generation drowning in technology. Some Christians complain that the wizard-in-training learned witchcraft at Hogwarts, but maybe if we had not lost our own wonder and mystery found in the pages of the Bible, children would not have been so hungry for what Harry's adventures had to offer them. What if Christ followers had shown Harry's fans the mystery of God's work and the realities of the spiritual realm? What if we had told of angels, the Evil One's plan to destroy good people, talking animals, and fire falling from the sky with the same wonder and mystery Rowling shows in telling her story? I am grateful for director Peter Jackson's portrayal of J. R. R. Tolkien's *Lord of the Rings* trilogy, in which he brought new life to the battle between good and evil told in the mysteries of Middle Earth and in a time before our own. We too often fear what God has already defeated, and we ignore what God has given us to live lives of adventure and wonder.

I am drawn to nature in my search for wonder. I grew up on the coastal plains of Southeast Texas. My parents moved from the plains of the Texas Panhandle only to settle on the flatlands of the Gulf Coast. No wonder I longed for the heights of mountains. The tallest thing around my part of the world as a child was a pine tree. Trips to the mountains are still trips of awe for me. I once spoke for a conference at Hume Lake, California, in the conference center at the Sequoia National Forest. I thought I had seen big pines in Colorado and New Mexico, but nothing compares to the majesty of the Sequoias. As I walked around and through the General Grant and Lee trees, I marveled at God's handiwork. Their age and height challenged any perceptions of time and natural size I could comprehend. To stand at the base of a Giant Sequoia was to know my smallness in the grand scheme of things. To stand before an angel of God is more wondrous still. I am a naturalist in Gary Thomas' *Sacred Pathways* scheme of how we relate to the divine. No man-made cathedral can match the beauty and majesty of a sanctuary formed in the wilds of nature. Stained glass windows and theater lighting pale in comparison to sunlight that dances through a canopy of aspen and birch in autumn.

GABRIEL'S TRIP TO MARY

An angel announced Samson's and Jesus' births. God wanted their parents to know he had special plans for their boys. Both were chosen by God to be a savior for his people. Both were born for a purpose. Like the child's mother, the messenger who announced Samson's birth was nameless. Gabriel himself came to Mary. This is the same mighty angel who left heaven to explain a vision to Daniel, the same angel who told Zechariah, "I stand in the presence of God, and I have been sent to tell you this good news."[9] While a no-name angel announced Samson's birth, God chose one close at his side to make Jesus' birth announcement.

Scripture only mentions Gabriel twice; once on his trip to Daniel, a second time on a journey to announce the conceptions of John and Jesus' birth. Each time God sent him into the lives of those God had chosen to rescue his people. I wonder if there is anything about Daniel's ministry in exiled Israel and Mary's presence in Roman-occupied Israel that caused God to choose Gabriel among the millions of messengers at his disposal. I suppose precarious times demanded a courier who would not fail. I picture Gabriel getting God's message and leaving the throne room of God. As he makes his way toward creation, the chatter among the angelic courtiers passes the news throughout heaven that the Plan had begun; Gabriel was on his way to announce God's plan of salvation to humans. As he powered past the realm of God's throne, demons may have picked up his scent and reported to headquarters the Son's invasion of earth had begun. The battle was about to escalate. Gabriel delivered the message that God was about to complete his redemptive plan.

In Luke 1:26–38, Gabriel materialized before a young unwed teenager. She was engaged, but unlike Samson's mother, she was a virgin who did not know if she would or could bare children. Her life was still before her and all the hopes that were born in childhood dreams were alive as real possibilities. While an angel quenched the bitterness of barrenness for Manoah's wife and gave her hope to live on, Gabriel shattered the hopes and dreams of Mary. Pregnancy before marriage was not acceptable in God-honoring families.

Gabriel began his message to Mary with an assurance that God favored her rather than starting with the stark truth like the angel did with Samson's mother. "Greetings, you who are highly favored! The LORD is with you."[10] Like Daniel before her who had fainted upon seeing Gabriel, Mary was disturbed by this mighty being from God's presence. Her emotions and thoughts stumbled like a toddler to hold on to something in order to stay on her feet. Where Manoah's wife had seemed almost nonchalant about the angel's presence, calmly telling her husband of her visitor, Mary was troubled. Gabriel must have seen the wonder and fear in the teenager's eyes. He continued,

> Do not be afraid, Mary, you have found favor with God. You will be with child and give birth to a son, and you are to give him the name Jesus. He will be great and will be called Son of the Most High. The Lord God will give him the throne of his father David, and he will reign over the house of Jacob forever; his kingdom will never end.

God had big plans for Mary. She would be the birth mother of God's Son, the Promised One of the Ages. The reign of God through David would be restored. Who wouldn't say yes to that invitation? Most girls expected to become mothers, but the mother of the "Son of the Most High"? Her mind started to wonder about the meaning of the message when the left side of her brain spoke up, "One problem: the I-haven't-had-sex-yet part doesn't fit here." Reality challenged revelation. So, she asked, "How will this be since I am a virgin?"

"Fair question from a human," Gabriel may have thought. But he was prepared for her earth-bound point of view, and he explained,

> "The Holy Spirit will come upon you, and the power of the Most High will overshadow you. So the holy one to be born will be called the Son of God . . . nothing is impossible with God."

His answer certainly didn't clear things up completely, but it seems to have been enough for Mary. Rather than asking more questions, Mary submitted to God's purpose, saying, "I am the Lord's servant. May it be to me as you have said." Mary, like Samson's mother, accepted her place in God's plans. Through these women, two saviors entered the stage of human history.

Two angels came to two women bearing testimony to two births, two sons who were saviors, and all this set the stage for what would seem to be parallel lives used by God. The first would begin "the deliverance of Israel from the hands of the Philistines"[11]; the second would "reign over the house of Jacob forever; his kingdom will never end."[12] Samson, a Nazirite; Jesus, a Nazarene—both set apart for God. But from the announcements of their births forward, their life paths parted, and their lives were only echoes of each other. Only one would complete his divine purpose as designed by God. Only one would live for others rather than use his prowess and strength for himself. Only one would choose to die for the sake of others. Only one would be the once-for-all Savior.

DISCUSSION QUESTIONS

1. What accommodations have Christians made with the culture that could potentially be a compromise in their relationship with God? How have churches done the same?

2. What are some "little g" gods that are part of our culture? How do they keep us from trusting God completely?

3. How has your faith deepened when you did not get what you thought was best for you and your family?

4. What do you know about angels? What information from the Bible was new for you as you seek to understand these spiritual beings?

5. How were Samson and Jesus' birth announcements similar? How were they different? What do those differences tell you about who they are?

6. What do the purposes of Samson and Jesus' lives tell you about the Plan
    of God to rescue the hearts of all people?

Chapter Two

CONVINCING DAD

O Lord, I beg you, let the man of God you sent to us come again to
teach us how to bring up the boy who is to be born.

—JUDGES 13:8

I'm a pushover when it comes to discipline and my daughters. My wife, Kim, and I warred most when the girls were teenagers. We never argued over our core values. Our battles were over matters of preference like eating habits, hair, clothes, grades, and pressure to succeed. We are dissimilar in our personalities, and we are different in many of our desires for our children. As in many families with daughters, Mom sometimes becomes the hard line on some matters, while Dad is easier to convince.

My daughters did not need long arguments to convince me to get their way. They knew I would not budge on character issues, but I was weak when it came to decisions about food, curfews, and friends. We would sneak dessert when we ate without their mother. I was often asleep when they came in on Saturday nights, and I had a hard time keeping up with their friends' names. But they knew when I would not compromise and that their mother and I shared decisions on the major things about their lives. Yet too many times, they could simply ask in their little girl voices, and I would give them what they wanted. My daughters still can turn my heart with a look.

Convincing Dad is part of our tale of two saviors. Not that God needed the fathers to accomplish his purposes, but God graciously included them in the plans for their sons. God wanted commitment from the men who would influence the boys who would become saviors for his people.

INSTRUCTIONS TO DADS

Joseph's fiancée and Manoah's wife accepted their divine callings and went on with their lives as their children grew in their wombs. Samson's father received the news of his son's conception and destiny from his barren wife. He didn't bat an eye when his wife told him of the man of God's visit and message. Her explanation of the appearance and origin of the messenger seemed to satisfy him. What moved him to prayer was the message that his son would be a Nazirite who was to "drink no wine or other fermented drink and . . . not eat anything unclean . . . from birth until the day of his death." Those things were probably part of the family diet, and he may have been hard put to eliminate them from the dinner table. The the Nazirite lifestyle was rigorous, and Manoah had to be intimidated about raising a Nazirite child. But his wife doesn't seem to have been as startled by the news; instead, she calmly accepted her role in bringing this child into the world.

Manoah wanted help with God's plan. Like a good father who is responsible for the spiritual, physical, emotional, and intellectual development of his children, Manoah's first prayer was "O Lord, I beg you, let the man of God you sent to us come again to teach us how to bring up the boy who is to be born." He wanted instructions on how to raise his son. Visitation by an angel was one thing. Parenting a boy set apart for God was something completely different.

Manoah's prayer is that of every potential parent. I remember the night Kim's water broke with our first child. Her pregnancy had been normal. We had completed the circuit of baby showers and Lamaze classes, but the birth seemed like a distant dream to me. I never thought about it much and went on with life as normally as I could. Women don't have the same advantage as men do to ignore a pregnancy. Every time the child moves in her womb, every contraction is a reminder from the child: "I'm coming, ready or not."

When Kim called out from the bathroom, "My water just broke," it was about 11:00 at night. I was ready for bed, not a birth. We moved into execution mode like Homeland Security headquarters when the nation's terrorist alert goes from yellow to red. After a flurry of stuffing clothes and our other stock-piled supplies in suitcases, we started our thirty-minute drive downtown to the hospital. All I remember saying the entire way was, "Oh, no. Oh, no. We're having a baby." Kim remembers my mantra a little differently, but I'm sticking to my version.

We arrived at the hospital and the birthing experience began. I admit we worshipped the little-g god of technology in the form of an epidural that night. Pain is not something Kim cares to tolerate in any way. At 4:15 a.m., I held in my arms the most beautiful baby girl ever born. Later that day, while mother and daughter were sleeping in the room, I prayed like Manoah, "Lord, I have no clue how to do this. Please show me the way." I think most fathers pray that prayer. Out of fear or humility or both, fathers turn to their Father to seek the wisdom to mold and guide their children's lives.

God heard Manoah's prayer and sent the messenger back to his wife. He came to her while she was out in the field. She was the only one who could iden-tify the angelic being. When the angel reappeared before her, she ran to her hus-band and cried, "He's here! The man who appeared to me the other day!" She wasn't crazy. Lightning does strike twice in the same place.

She led Manoah to the man of God still standing in the field. He approached his divine guest and asked, "Are you the one who talked to my wife?" I'm not sure of the tone of his voice but Manoah seemed to be a macho guy—espe-cially if his genes produced a physical specimen like Samson. There could have been a threatening tone to his question. After all, how dare this guy tell his wife and not Manoah that he would have a son and be required to live accord-ing to strict, disruptive rules. In that culture, men addressed men. News like this shouldn't travel through his wife—or so he might well have thought. The angel answered curtly, "I am." I assume his voice had a mighty sound. You don't threaten an angel on mission from God by puffing up your chest and raising your voice. Imagine Manoah's hair standing on end at the sound of the angel's supernatural voice. Or, it may have been the mention of "I am" that caused him to stand with unease.

I AM, as we are used to reading, *is* the name of God. God *is.* All that *is* emanates from God. I AM is life and to speak the name is to worship, to honor, to call upon the source of all that exists in the universe. To speak the name of God is no light matter. Power ripples across space when those who trust that God both "exists and cares enough to respond to those who seek him"[13] summon I AM. The God of the Universe offered the name to Moses when he called the royal-boy-turned-murderer-turned-shepherd to lead Israel's tribes out of Egypt. Later, God reminded Moses of the power of the name by insisting that the Israelites were not to use the name of God in careless ways.[14] God's name is so sacred that Jews do not speak it at all but use names like Adonai and Jehovah instead. I AM on the lips of a celestial being is holy enough to silence any mortal. The sound of the angel's simple "I am" [the one who was here earlier] must have sounded enough like the name of Manoah's God that he lowered his shoulders and stood down.

We no longer respect the name of God. Jesus, Christ, and God have become street talk for common people. "Oh, my God!" is no longer a prayer but a term of exclamation, something like "I can't believe it!" Most no longer use the name of Jesus to invoke the Holy One; "Christ" belongs to the lyrics of rappers and scripts of movie stars. Somewhere along the path to prosperity and self-aggrandizement we lost respect for the One who brought us wealth and created in us the freedom to choose for ourselves. I AM no longer quiets the hearts of those who have turned from the holy to the mundane to find purpose in life. But the day will come, the Word promises, when "at the name of Jesus every knee should bow in heaven and on earth and under the earth, and every tongue confess that Jesus is Lord, to the Glory of God the Father."[15] I AM will reign in the hearts of men—if not now, certainly in eternity.

CONFIRMATION AND INVITATION

Manoah asked the angel, "When your words are fulfilled, what is to be the rule for the boy's life and work?" He knew the answer. His wife had told him, but he wanted to hear it himself. Manoah is like those who hear a clear word of the Lord on the lips of someone else but insist they hear the same message directly from God. How many times have you heard from a friend or spiritual mentor that you should give up a bad habit? You know your friend is right, but you keep going with the false premise that if God wanted you to stop going, God would tell you to your face. We are naïve to think we would rather hear directly from God.

The angel's response was, "Your wife must do all that I have told her. She must not eat anything that comes from the grapevine, nor drink any wine or other fermented drink nor eat anything unclean. She must do everything I have commanded her." He answered Manoah's question by restating what he told Manoah's wife. Clearly, Manoah did not give enough credence to what his wife told him, but the angel refused to do anything more than affirm what he had already said. Manoah's disrespect for his wife as a messenger of God will show up later in how his son treated women. Sons learn from their fathers the value of women in their lives. God, on the other hand, felt it sufficient to bring the news of his work to the nameless woman who would bear the savior of God's people.

Either the angel stated his message convincingly or Manoah became enamored with the awesome nature of the man before him, but in the end, Manoah was satisfied the message was authentic. Manoah invited the man of God to join his household for a meal of goat. Sharing a meal in the ancient world was a serious act of fellowship. Abraham offered his divine guests a meal, as did Gideon. It's what you did for special guests. But along with his act of honor toward his guest, Manoah wanted to hear more from this one who spoke for God. He also wanted to hear more about the nature of his son's life as a savior of God's people. Manoah would have known the stories of Ehud, Deborah, and Gideon—men and women who had defeated the enemies of God and kept the Promised Land for Israel. His boy would be a legend. Generations would remember his son's greatness. Manoah wanted to hear more.

The angel politely declined the invitation to eat. He had done his job and was ready to return to the presence of God. Earth and humans were not his usual hangout. Like an American ambassador sent to deliver a communiqué from Washington to a foreign administration, this messenger was ready to return to familiar surroundings. He would have stories to tell around the throne that night. He excused himself, "Even if I stay, I won't eat your food. But if you want to prepare a Whole-Burnt-Offering for GOD, go ahead—offer it!" He directed Manoah's efforts away from his stomach to the worship of God. Why waste a good goat for a meal? Kill and cook it for a higher purpose. Sacrifice it as a "Whole-Burnt-Offering for GOD" instead of a four-course meal for yourself.

A burnt offering was one way a Nazirite became clean when defiled by being in the presence of a dead person during his time of separation.[16] Maybe the messenger knew such an offering would be needed often in the life of God's chosen one. Maybe he knew it would not be long before Samson's father would need to make such a sacrifice for his son's encounter with a dead lion.

An Angel Called "Beyond Understanding"

Manoah, not knowing the man was an angel, ventured into the being's personal space and asked him his name. Manoah said he wanted to know "so that we may honor your name when your word comes true." I have not figured out Manoah's motive here. If he was sincere, then he desired to give God credit as his boy became a hero for God. On the other hand, if he tried to stack up evidence to convince his buddies down at the grain co-op that he was not crazy or that he was more favored by God than they were, then I would say his motives were selfish. The more powerful names we attach to our stories make us more believable. True faith, however, trusts the raw word of those sent to us and we wait to watch that word unfold, with or without endorsement from others.

The angel answered, "Why do you ask my name? It is beyond understanding," from the root *pala'* which means "wonderful." His answer was more like Jesus' answer to James and John when they asked to sit at his right and left hand when he came into his kingdom. "You don't know what you are asking," Jesus told them.[17] The disciples were clueless to the implications of their inquiry. So was Manoah. Humans are mysterious enough for those who travel from eternal dimensions into this one,[18] but I doubt the angel wanted to understand how they reasoned when he asked, "Why do you ask my name?" Like a grandfather patting his grandson's head knowing if he told the truth, the small child would be unable to comprehend the words, the angel simply smiled and said, "It is beyond understanding."

King David used a similar Hebrew word for the idea of something "beyond understanding" when he pondered how God knew his movements and his thoughts before he spoke them. The Shepherd King confessed that when he became aware of all of this it was too wonderful, beyond understanding, inconceivable.[19] All that was left for David after meditating on God's greatness was to accept that God was more than his mind could comprehend or his imagination could ever devise. He found hope and solace in the depth of God. He did not fear; he trusted. True saints have no need to minimize the mystery of God. They rest in its reality. God-chasers thrive in the certainty they will never know the completeness of the One who has called them to serve, worship, and join in mission with him.

"Beyond understanding" was the essence of the angel sent to proclaim the good news to Manoah and his wife. For David, it was good to know his God was beyond his experience and one in whom he could place his ultimate trust. But Manoah and his wife did not know God the way David did.

DISCUSSION QUESTIONS _____

1. If you are a mother or a father, what were your first feelings and thoughts when you found out you were going to be a parent? What were your fears and anticipations when you first held your child?

2. Manoah wanted to hear the message of God firsthand. How are you like him? Are you okay with two-party information about God's Word to you—like that of a preacher, conference leader, or author—or do you insist on knowing God's message firsthand?

3. How are our attitudes toward the name of God different than those of the biblical characters who knew him? How has this change in respect in the name of God affected our attitude toward God?

4. What does the angel's answer to Manoah's request to know his name, "Beyond understanding," tell you about the angel and God?

Chapter Three

AN ANGEL IN THE FLAME

As the flame blazed up from the altar toward heaven,
the angel of the Lord ascended in the flame.

—JUDGES 13:20

Fire fascinates me. The ancients saw it as one of the four elements, the building blocks of all things. Witches and preachers still acknowledge its power and its symbol for things spiritual. I am enamored with the mystery of burning things, from a candle to a pile of cleared trees on the farm. Fire, energy released from that which burns, is a source of light, warmth, and power. When channeled appropriately, it supports life. When it rages outside its boundaries, it takes life. Man's experiment with fire has brought us both the soft light of a candlelight meal and the horrors of Hiroshima.

I remember standing outside one winter's night, watching a friend's house burn. He had called after midnight to say his family was safe, but his house was in flames. All his material possessions rose as sparks above the lawn he had mowed that morning. When I arrived, the fire trucks' lights danced off the houses as smoke and steam floated into the dry, cold air. It looked like a scene from *Apocalypse Now*.

Mark was calm. His faith stood on the certainty of God's provision in his life. He had grown to trust God's presence in all that happened in life. For over twenty-five years, his mother and father had mentored him in radical faith while serving the people of Honduras as missionaries. Hurricanes, drought, and poverty had never chased God from the scene. Why should a house fire in suburban Dallas take God away now?

Mark had prepared for Y2K, but he had not planned on his house burning down. He had fifty-five-gallon drums of water, canned goods, and his first gun, which he purchased in case of crisis. As we stood with the exhaust of the fire truck's diesel engines warming our legs, Mark told me he had put ashes from that night's fire in the fireplace in the garage because it was too cold to put them outside. Ashes retain enough energy to start a house fire hours after the flame is gone. The smoke detectors beeped while the tires on his mother-in-law's car melted in the garage. Everyone got out safely, but every material thing was lost. Water and fire damaged what didn't burn. He would have to start over. Fire had taken his home *and* his preparations for the disaster of Y2K.

As ironic as it sounds, he stood on the brink of knowing God in ways he would have never known without the complete loss of all he owned. He would learn what giving and receiving meant. He would learn what "fellowship of the saints" felt like and what the Acts 2 church must have experienced as people served others and no one had need among them. Like setting fires to wheat fields in West Texas to ensure fertility in the growing season, the embers' ignition prepared the way for a fresh relationship with God.

Worship by Rote

On a much smaller scale, Manoah did not watch his house burn, but he saw his hopes for a cooked lunch end as his guest refused to eat with him. The angel asked him to offer the goat to God as a sacrifice. Manoah stopped asking questions and went about preparing the animal as his father had taught him. He built a fire and gathered grain to complete his gift to God. It was an offering of thankfulness for the child who would be born, an acknowledgement of God's grace and guidelines for his set-apart life. Manoah led the goat to a rock that protruded as a platform for worship. He cut the animal's throat, drained its life-giving blood, and placed its body pieces on the fire. Manoah and his wife watched as goat flesh burned in the flame of sacrifice.

These two Israelites worshipped because they had been told to worship; sacrifice by command. They wanted to eat dinner, but the angel called them to worship. When asked, they followed the protocol of sacrifice and stood faithful to pray what they had always prayed and to hear what they had always heard. Their lips moved in cadence with the rite. Their hearts never beat faster than the tradition of their faith. The angel watched as they went through the motions. He may have missed true worship around the King in heaven, thinking, "Humans have no clue what they are missing."

The sizzle of burning flesh was nothing new to these worshippers' ears. The smell of cooking meat made their mouths water. A by-product of worship in those days was a cooked meal. Sacrifice, however, had become as regular as setting a meal for the family. Manoah had moved seamlessly from "How about some dinner?" to sacrificing the main course to God. Modern Christians move as thoughtlessly the other direction. They worship God and then move to lunch at the local restaurant as naturally as Manoah shifted his focus from dinner around the table to watching sparks fly to heaven.

An Angel in the Flame

Something amazing happened in the routine of their worship: "As the flame blazed up from the altar toward heaven, the angel of the Lord ascended in the flame."

An angel in the flame! The angel stepped from earth into the flame of sacrifice. He climbed from the ground onto the altar. He was not consumed but transported. He was not burnt but carried with the sparks riding on heat torrents rising from the fire. Flesh, fire, and spirit rose to the Creator carrying God's messenger into eternity like seagulls riding the wild winds at the Cliffs of Moher on the coast of Ireland. The spirit being who had stood with the worshippers and who had spoken human language suddenly evaporated into the flames toward heaven. An angel rose in the flame of sacrifice into the presence of the One who had sent him.

Why does it amaze us that things earthly and things eternal mingle so closely together? Why do we wonder when eternity enters earth or the other way around? Isn't heaven closer to earth than we think? Didn't Paul tell us we are to seek those things unseen rather than those seen because the unseen realities are the ones that are real? When the Nephilim intermarried with the women of earth, there were fewer boundaries between the natural and supernatural. Nuclear scientists do not doubt the nearness of infinity to time, space, and mass. Why do we doubt God enters our world, mingles, and exits in Spirit? Have our eyes become too accustomed to the darkness of the material to entertain the brightness of the eternal?

The angel-in-the-flame departure was more than a supernatural trick, like one of the X-Men's mutant maneuvers. He was not showing off as he parted. He simply did what angels do. He left this foreign realm for the familiar. We must remember Scripture records only those things that reveal God to those who seek him. So why an exit like this one in a story of a savior? Could it have been a reminder of the pillar of fire in the wilderness that signaled the presence of God to the Jewish parents? Or was it simply the angel's playful move to return to home?

Elijah departed this world in a chariot of fire,[20] but this pre-NASA launch into eternity is the only biblical record of an angel exiting in a flame. Mirroring God's messengers who gathered in the night when Jesus was born to confirm the divine nature of his birth to Mary via the shepherds, this angel departed in a supernatural way to let those who had heard his message know that his words were true.

The Picture of a Life

The angel in the flame was a foreshadowing of Samson's life. Israel's leader was set apart for the purposes of God, empowered with muscle, looks, and wit to rescue God's people from their enemies. He was to be a savior, a hero, and leader. He had divine promise and presence to ensure his success. As long as he stayed within God's plan and Spirit, he would have the power to serve God's purposes for his birth and life. Step outside the plan, and he would fall to earth like Lucifer after his failed coup in heaven.

The flame of ego rather than God's Spirit consumed Samson. We will see how the Spirit of the Lord came upon him to empower him, but in the end his life flamed out in self-interest. His life became a pyre of pride that devoured all potential for ending well. Samson could not live apart from his lusts and selfish desires. He never let his life be a sacrifice to his Maker. Manoah's goat did a better job at that holy task than the massive strong man.

Fire marked the beginning of his life, but stone marked his death. The pile of temple stones he eventually crumbled in his final murder-suicide could have been an altar upon which he sacrificed his life for others, like the rock upon which Manoah laid the goat, but he chose to bring down the house to avenge the bad things he believed had happened to him. God may have desired to bring his servant home via a flame elevator, but Samson would not let himself go that way. As strong in will as in muscle, he chose to end his life just as he chose to live it. Humility was not a hallmark of either his life or death.

Me?

God created you and me to be messengers of his love to others. The New Testament called *apostoloi,* the sent ones, those whom Jesus sent into the world as his messengers.[21] God designed our lives for service to the King and for worship of his glory. God's Spirit is the flame that envelops us, that indwells us. Paul asked the rhetorical question, "Do you not know that your body is a temple of the Holy Spirit, who is in you, whom you have received from God?"[22] The Flame of the Spirit sets up residence in those who open the door of their hearts to his invitation.

A life captured and directed by God is one wrapped in the flame of His Spirit and set apart to accomplish divine purposes. The apostle Paul described our lives consumed by the glory of God as "living sacrifices, holy and pleasing to God."[23] We are to be walking, breathing, flame-shrouded followers of Jesus, giving light, love, and hope to others, inflamed in God's Presence. Sparks should fly from our lives; sparks that come from the energy of messengers consumed by the One who sent them. Christ followers run into life with their hearts lit by the One who called them and who gave them a reason to live. We are the "light of the world" because Christ's flame burns within us. We live with "nothing between us and God, our faces shining with the brightness of his face."[24]

Stephen, the first martyr of the Jesus movement, lived a life aflame with Christ's Spirit. Dr. Luke tells us the religious leaders remember seeing him and that they "stared at Stephen because his face became as bright as an angel's."[25] Stephen had a shining face because, unlike Moses' veiled face as he descended from Mt. Sinai, this deacon's unveiled face reflected the flame of Christ's Spirit. He appeared angelic—a man wrapped in the fire of God's Presence. Stones killed Stephen like they would Samson, but the flame of God's Spirit shone on Stephen's face as earth's stones took his life. Samson's face, as I read the story, had no such glow.

Stephen was God's messenger who spoke the truth about Jesus to those who could not see that Jesus was the Sent One. They stoned Stephen like they crucified Jesus—as another threat to their traditions and lives of power. I want to die not with Samson's strength, but with Stephen's shining face.

Yet, no matter the divine promise, angelic pledge, or heavenly presence of God in our lives, we, like Samson, tend to live for ourselves. Flames of lust, greed, and image consume us. Like Samson, we step away from the flame of God's Spirit to pursue the fires of other tribes, and we too often find ourselves under a pile of stones we brought down upon ourselves. God created us to be his messengers, his *apostoloi,* clothed in his Spirit. We, however, live like we would rather die at our own hand than risk living in God's hands. Is there any hope we will *not* live our lives like Samson?

JESUS, THE ANGEL IN THE FLAME

Jesus, our Rescuer and Leader, "gave himself up for us as a fragrant offering and sacrifice to God."[26] Jesus was the Angel in the Flame. He was God's Sent One, shrouded in God's Presence; God as Messenger. Jesus proclaimed the coming of the kingdom of heaven. He taught us about his Father in heaven and how if we love God first and others second, we all can live together. Jesus was all that was eternal and all that was temporal, the perfect mix of spirit and flesh. He moved from eternal existence to walk on the earth and speak in a language we all understand. He was an ambassador of the kingdom of heaven and deputized his followers to live as if they were ambassadors, too. He taught us

"God is spirit, and his worshipers must worship in spirit and in truth."[27] All the material trappings we build around our praise to God are no more than the mountain the Samaritan woman posed to Jesus as a place of worship, not a way of worship.

The purposes of the One who sent him consumed Jesus' life. Sparks flew from his hands as he healed the sick. Light clothed him on the mountaintop with Moses, Elijah, and his three closest followers. His glory shone as he gathered children to himself, and he burned with righteous anger at the hypocrisy of religious leaders. Jesus promised when he ascended into heaven he would send his Spirit, the Holy Flame for all of us. And he did. With "a sound like the blowing of a violent wind," we are told that what seemed to be tongues of fire . . . came to rest on each of them" who had gathered to pray on the day of Pentecost.[28] That event ignited the *ekklesia*, the church, with the flame of Christ's Spirit and empowered them to carry out the commission Jesus had given them to complete.

Unlike Samson's, Jesus' death was not to avenge those who treated him unjustly; Jesus died to free all people from their own bondage to sin. He could have brought down the temple on those who beat him, like Samson did to those who put out his eyes, but Jesus' heart was broken even for those who tortured him. Samson never got to that place in his life, and this is why Samson did not fulfill his full calling as a savior. He could only be called a judge. Jesus will be known as the Judge.

AFTER THE ANGEL ASCENDS

Our storyteller described the worshippers' reactions to the angel in the flame: "Manoah and his wife fell with their faces to the ground." Things as wonderful as supernatural occurrences throw us to the ground. All we can do is hide our faces in the dirt and pray we are not singed by its glory. With their faces "to the ground"—a position of worship we have lost in modern evangelical liturgy as we stand to worship in song—Manoah and his wife now understood the name that was beyond understanding. They "realized that it was the angel of the LORD" who had visited them. The mystery was revealed, yet it only produced more mystery. Like Isaiah in the smoke-filled temple with seraphim flying over his head who cried, "Woe to me!"[29] they could only assume doom was their fate for having been in the presence of the Holy.

Manoah was the first to speak, "We are doomed to die! We have seen God!" An angel in the flame surely signaled God's presence. Nothing else could account for such a scene. They would have known about God's conversation with Moses where God had told the shepherd-turned-leader, "No one may see Me [God] and live."[30] If Moses, who was so close to God, could not see God, how was Manoah to survive such a meeting? Moses survived the passing of God only as he hid in a crevice and got a glimpse of God's back. Manoah believed the word passed down through his ancestors, and he prepared for his death.

Once again, his wife was the levelheaded, faith-filled one. She reasoned, "If the Lord had meant to kill us, he would not have accepted a burnt offering and grain offering from our hands, nor shown us all these things or now told us this." If God were one to strike down those to whom he had sent an angel, they would have been dead a long time ago. No, the angel in the flame was validation that all that was said before was true. They could begin to prepare for their child.

CONVINCING JESUS' STEPFATHER

An angel announced Jesus' birth to Joseph, Mary's fiancé. Gabriel, like the angel whose name was beyond understanding, went to the man who would parent the soon-to-be-Savior. Joseph did not get an angelic visit to prepare him for Mary's pregnancy; he seems to have learned through the social network of the day. All Matthew 1 tells us is that she became pregnant "before they came together." While Luke gave us reason to believe that Joseph was in on some of the conversations between Mary and Elizabeth and that he had heard Zechariah's story of naming John, Matthew pictures Joseph knowing nothing about Mary's pregnancy until her pregnancy pushed her robe out so far she could hide it no longer.

Joseph's response to his fiancée's condition showed some compassion. He "did not want to expose her to public disgrace," so he planned to "divorce her quietly" and get on with his carpentry career. Matthew describes him as a "righteous man." Joseph wanted to live an upright life, and his fiancée's infidelity would not cause him to make a public exhibition of her.

When God saw Joseph's heart moving in the direction of divorce, he sent an angel to calm his spirit. This time, a nameless messenger of God materialized in Joseph's dream and explained things. The message was clear and simple:

> Do not be afraid to take Mary as your wife, because what is conceived in her is from the Holy Spirit. She will give birth to a son, and you are to give him the name Jesus because he will save his people from their sins.

The angel went on to remind Joseph that the prophet Isaiah had promised the Savior would be born of a virgin and that his name, "Immanuel," would mean "God with us." Joseph was to marry his pregnant fiancée because what was going on was supernatural, purposed by God, and prophesied centuries before. Joseph, like every Jewish father before him, was to name his son. It would be *Jesus*: Yeshua, Savior, and Rescuer.

When he woke from his angel encounter, Matthew tells us Joseph "did what the angel of the Lord had commanded him and took Mary home as his wife." Obedience followed hearing, and the purposes of God continued.

Two men encountered angels with messages about their wives and future sons. Two men whose God had chosen them to be part of the redemptive adventure. Two men who trusted God's word and went about doing what God told them to do. As we will see, Manoah was a different father to Samson than Joseph was to Jesus. Their earthly fathers influenced both saviors, and the differences would be realized early in their lives.

Discussion Questions _____

1. How do you see your life as "an angel in the flame" of God's presence? What does the metaphor teach you about how God sees your life?

2.   Honestly assess your life as one who is sent by Christ into the world. Is it more like the description of Stephen's face at his death or like Samson at the end of his life?

3.   Compare Jesus' life and death and Samson's life and death. How are they different as "an angel in the flame," and how are they the same?

4.   What were the differences between Joseph's and Manoah's responses to the angels who came to them? Which one is more like you?

Chapter Four

BOYS WILL BE BOYS

. . . the Spirit of the Lord began to stir him.

—JUDGES 13:25

You may have received the following story as it was passed around the Internet—the twenty-first century tribal fire for telling stories. A mother was preparing pancakes for her sons, Kevin, five, and Ryan, three. The boys began to argue over who would get the first pancake. Their mother saw the opportunity for a moral lesson. "If Jesus were sitting here, He would say, 'Let my brother have the first pancake, I can wait.'" Kevin turned to his younger brother and said, "Ryan, you be Jesus!" Boys will be boys, and sharing is not always a natural habit for any child.

Jesus' and Samson's biographers briefly survey the births and childhoods of both saviors. We don't hear much about their table conversations at three and five, but we do get a brief glimpse into their formative years. Jesus, for obvious reasons, has many more pages about his birth than Samson, even though coverage of his birth occupies a fraction of the space devoted to the rest of his ministry. It's not where you begin life but where you finish the race that determines how you are remembered. Still, beginnings set the stage for life, so the stories of people's lives tell of birthplaces and early accounts of childhood.

"The woman gave birth to a boy and named him Samson." That's nearly all that is said about Samson's birth and childhood. Manoah's wife gave birth to a boy like the angel had said she would, and she gave him his name. Manoah may have had a say in naming his son, but our storyteller only mentions Mom as the giver of the name. Maybe Manoah already had returned to the stuff of life and let his wife do all the family work, including naming his only son. He seems to have checked out after the birth of his child, and in the text to come, we will see a boy whose potential never is released under the mentoring of a caring father.

The angel in the flame did not prescribe a name for Israel's savior, so Manoah's wife came up with her own name for the child. The name Samson is from the Hebrew root for the sun (*shemesh*). Some have also tried to link it to the names of Babylonian and Greek heroes, but our best bet is the Hebrew form of the name.

Why that name? Maybe she saw him as the sun of her life—a bright hope born in her barren years. Maybe she wanted the other mothers in her tribe to know her boy was brighter than theirs. Who among his peers could have a name bigger than "the sun"? The boy would be powerful with both the God of Israel and the god of the sun on his side. Samson's naturalistic name shows how God's people often honored the temporal above their Creator.

After giving his name, in a breath the writer tells us, "He grew and the Lord blessed him." "He grew" is an understatement. In the next verses, he emerges as a hulk of a man who can tear a lion in half like a goat—as if any normal man could do that! He must have been some boy; head and shoulders above his peers, stronger than an ox, and sporting his thick head of hair, uncut hair since his birth. And, "the Lord blessed him." He grew and God blessed his growth. God made good on his promise before his parents' eyes. That's all we know about Samson's childhood. But something did not happen during those formative years, and this failure will become part of the reason that he never fulfilled all God birthed him to be. We will discover that fatal weakness when we read about his decision to marry.

Jerusalem's Child

Joseph named Jesus. After a miraculous birth attended by armies of angels, a flock of shepherds, and a caravan of magicians from the East, Joseph dedicated and circumcised his son in the temple according to the practice of God's people. Unlike Manoah, Joseph carried out his role as Jesus' earthly father. Luke tells us, "On the eighth day, when it was time to circumcise him, he was named Jesus, the name the angel had given him before he had been conceived." Here was Joseph's key role. He was a righteous father who followed the instructions of God to consecrate, name, and set apart his son according to the lineage of Abraham.

Luke summarizes Jesus' childhood, "the child grew and became strong; he was filled with wisdom, and the grace of God was upon him." Like Samson, he "grew and became strong, and the grace of God was upon him." Both saviors were part of God's plans to rescue his people and to redeem them back to him. God blessed and graced them both.

One phrase that describes Jesus is different from his Old Covenant counterpart. Luke adds, "he was filled with wisdom," and in the story that follows Jesus' dedication we see how a boy of twelve confounded those much older than him. In contrast, we don't hear about wisdom as one of Samson's character traits, and as we watch his life unfold, we never read that wisdom is part of the package. Solomon wrote that "the beginning of wisdom is the fear of the Lord." Jesus and Samson were different in this way. Jesus clearly honored his mother and father and revered his Father in heaven. Jesus embodied the essence of wisdom as he taught and ministered.

When Jesus was twelve and on one of his family's trips to Jerusalem for Passover he stayed behind as the caravan headed back home. He became so entangled in conversation with those who claimed to know his Father that he lost all track of time and missed roll call. A day into the journey home, his parents realized he was not with the traveling party, and they returned to find him. The last place most parents would look for a twelve-year-old boy would be in a place of worship. It took Mary and Joseph three days to turn to that possibility.

They found Jesus in the temple courts surrounded by his elders, talking about the things of God. When Mary approached and scolded him, Jesus acted surprised that they would worry about him, saying, "Didn't you know I had to be in my Father's house?" His question suggested that Mary had forgotten, at least for a moment, all that happened at his birth and the stories she probably had told him about his mission as Savior to God's people. I picture her giving him that look only mothers can give, because next thing we know, he followed his mother and father home to Nazareth where he continued to mature in every area of his life. Just as centuries before God had blessed Samson, the warrior, a muscle-bound boy with long hair, so now God blessed both Jesus, the Teacher, an honor student at age twelve.

HUMBLE BEGINNINGS

As our two heroes grew physically, the purposes of God began to play out in their lives. Samson grew up in "Mahaneh-dan, which is located between the towns of Zorah and Eshtaol." Mahaneh-dan was a small town with little significance in the history of Israel except for being where Samson grew up. It was something like what Hope, Arkansas, is to the history of America. Hope is the home of our forty-second president, but it will never be recognized like Washington, D.C. Samson's biographer does add that it was there that "the Spirit of the Lord began to stir him." Somewhere in the boy's playing, hunting, and maturing, God's Spirit began to take hold in the life of his chosen one. The Spirit of the Lord was the key to Samson's power and strength. He thought he could perform his mighty feats because of his physical power, but the biblical storyteller always lets us know it was God's Spirit that empowered Samson for his mighty acts. We become like Samson when we come to believe our cunning, wit, and reason are what get us what we have. Ultimately it is God, not us, who makes things happen.

Jesus followed his parents back to Nazareth, a no-name town in northern Israel. Like Mahaneh-dan, most of us would not know about Nazareth if it had not served as Jesus' hometown. When Philip told Nathaniel he had found "the one Moses wrote about in the Law, and about whom the Prophets also wrote— Jesus of Nazareth, the son of Joseph," Nathaniel responded, "Nazareth! Can anything good come from there?"[31] The town clearly had a hick reputation among the more sophisticated Israelites. How could God's Savior come from there? You would expect the Savior to come from a city like Jerusalem or at least

Shiloh, places God had designated as his own. But God confounds our guesses all the time—thus the need for faith—and he chose the off-the-beaten-path town of Nazareth as the place for his Chosen One's childhood.

I remember hearing Joel Barker, the Paradigm Man, describe how genuine change usually comes from the edges of an organization or culture. Seldom does someone in the existing paradigm bring the possibilities of a "paradigm shift" to the organization because he is too blinded by the current state to recognize new ways of seeing things. Barker mused that as he considered Jesus' life, that made sense to him that Jesus would bring a new way of relating to God from the edges of Israel: geographically from Nazareth, socially from Galilee, and religiously from someone outside the religious establishment. I think Mr. Barker is on to something.[32]

Both of our tales begin in small, off-the-map towns—towns more like Lincoln's Sinking Spring Farm in Kentucky than King Henry VIII's Greenwich, England. Lincoln's birthplace never became more than a historic park for curious citizens. King Henry's hometown became the location by which the world sets its clocks. Neither of our heroes' birthplaces has gained prominence in world history other than as the starting line of their lives' runs.

CORKY'S BOY

A small town grows up around people's lives. A suburb grows up around concrete paths. The first fosters interaction and relationships. The second requires effort to get outside your car and traffic patterns to meet your neighbors. The first has a downtown where people come in from outlying areas to buy essentials like food, clothes, and equipment. A suburb has no downtown; it has shopping centers that fit into platted neighborhoods, but there is no central gathering place. You can be anonymous in a suburb, known only to those to whom you choose to introduce yourself. You have no choice but to be known in a small town.

I remember growing up and going back to my parents' hometown in the panhandle town of Happy, Texas. Yes, home of the six-man football fighting Happy Cowboys. When the town still had about 350 residents, I would walk the town's streets and go into the different stores with my family. Sometimes I would go alone, especially to the corner drug store that still sported a soda fountain. I went in one day to order a chocolate malt, and the man behind the counter said, "Well, you must be Corky's boy." I smiled and answered, "Yes, sir. I am." Somehow word had gotten out that my father and his family were in town. My father's nickname was Corky—Corky, the Happy Cowboy. Now there's a small town beginning.

Jesus would have learned the ebb and flow of human life in his father's town of Nazareth. Neighbors may have brought broken things for Joseph to fix. Jesus may have gone on trips with his father to build in bigger cities. I assume he learned to make his own pieces of furniture and how to repair broken farm implements. I like the scene in Mel Gibson's *The Passion of the Christ* that portrayed Jesus making a table and chairs, even if the Western-style furniture is anachronistic. The Creator creating in a carpenter's shop should not be a surprise to us. I wonder how many objects Jesus invented just for the fun of it.

Samson and Jesus continued to mature, and we will watch them emerge into the public light as young men. Their births and childhoods are similar in several ways, but from the moments they each stepped onto the stage of life, they were very different. Life is clearly all about Samson as we watch him in chapter fourteen of Judges. Jesus is all about life when we see him approach John the Baptist at age thirty.

DISCUSSION QUESTIONS _____

1. Manoah and Joseph were involved in their sons' lives differently. Which one's involvement best reflects your father's presence in your life as a child?

2. Which parent named you? What does your name mean?

3. The Bible says Samson "grew and the Lord blessed him" and Jesus "grew in stature and in favor with God and man." How would you describe God's presence in your life? Would you say God blessed you or that you grew "in favor with God?"

4. Where did you grow up? How famous would you say it is? What happened there that played a role in your perception of God and his purposes for your life?

Chapter Five

THE LION AND THE LIONESS

Samson went down to Timnah and
saw there a young Philistine woman.

—JUDGES 14:1

John Eldredge describes a man who is *Wild At Heart* as one who will go in after the woman who wonders if she is worth fighting for and rescue her like a knight from the pages of King Arthur. A man offers his strength as a warrior for the woman so that she may realize her beauty. Not Samson. He simply saw a woman he liked, went home, and told his parents he had picked a bride like a teenager picks out his first car and that he would not listen to them until they got her for him. I wish it were that easy. Most men spend their teenage years and half of their twenties trying to find the woman they will love the rest of their lives. Samson saw, desired, demanded, and got what he wanted on the spot. History records, however, that the marriage didn't last more than a week, so I wouldn't recommend following Samson's example as the way to find your lifelong partner. Eldredge's idea has better results.

Samson's choice of his first wife gives us insight into his character and reveals something about how his parents trained him. Samson based his choice of wife on sight alone. No courtship, no romance, no sacrificial gestures to win her heart are part of this man-chooses-wife story. True, marriages were arranged then and offered nothing like the individual choices in today's cyber-world relationships. But the father usually did the arranging back then, not the son. We learn early in our tale that Samson called the shots with his parents, a warning sign of things to come.

He Saw a Woman

Our storyteller writes, "Samson went down to Timnah and saw there a young Philistine woman." We are not told they met or even talked. Samson saw her as he was passing through town and decided on the spot she was the one because when he got back home "he said to his father and mother, 'I have seen a Philistine woman in Timnah; now get her for me as my wife.'" The Hebrew word for "get her" also can mean "to capture or steal from." Samson wanted the girl, and he expected his parents to do whatever they needed to do to get her for him.

When I saw my wife for the first time, I was infatuated with her appearance. I don't know all the physiological and emotional reasons for that, but I know that when I saw her, my heart jumped, my mind raced, and I wanted to be as close as I could get to her. Yet she was not the only person I was attracted to by appearance alone—values, relationship, and discernment played a huge part in helping me know she was the one with whom I wanted to spend my life, over the others to whom I had been attracted. A two-year relationship before we married helped build the foundation for a lifelong partnership. Sight that is unfiltered through godly values, authentic relationship, and spiritual discernment fosters Samson's way of choosing a mate.

The apostle John, in his first letter to the Church, identified "the lust of the eyes" as coming not "from the Father but from the world."[33] He wanted his readers to know that the desires stirred up by sight are natural, but left unchecked, they take us to people and places that are not best for us. Keen eyesight is part of man's capacity to hunt. But what do you do with that ability when you no longer stalk prey but get your meat from the freezer at the grocery store? I have talked with men who said their obsession with pornography began with an e-mailed image that they did not solicit but could not get out of their mind. They soon found themselves chasing that image onto the Internet.

That hunt led to many other sights and sites that destroyed their relationships with real women.

Jesus warned, "The eye is the lamp of the body. If your eyes are good, your whole body will be full of light. But if your eyes are bad, your whole body will be full of darkness."[34] Jesus knew the power of sight. He knew its seductive power—especially in the attraction between men and women. Jesus taught that if your eyes were good in the sense that they look through God's lenses to what is best for your life, they would be filled with light. On the other hand, if you react to all you see, you can end up in some pretty dark places. Samson wore no protective lenses as he looked at the woman in Timnah that day. He wanted what he saw.

Samson's parents couldn't keep their son from making a bad choice. They had not trained him up with the filters needed to protect his decisions from the ultraviolet rays of lust. If they had done their job as parents, he may have taken the time to consider other options. Perhaps his parents spent more time telling him he couldn't cut his hair and all the other tedious rules of being a Nazirite than molding his character. Parenting by legalism—"do this, don't do that"—brings different results than parenting to mold a child's character. Read any of Philip Yancey's books. He'll tell you what the latter is like. Character that takes the time to wonder if a choice is right or wrong may have kept Samson from insisting he have the Philistine woman for his own.

When Samson insisted his parents go get the Philistine woman for him, they made an effort to guide him. They replied to his command, "Isn't there an acceptable woman among your relatives or among all our people? Must you go to the uncircumcised Philistines to get a wife?" Samson's mother and father knew from their parents that when God had given them a place in Canaan the rules of marriage were clear: "If you intermarry with them [the survivors of these nations that remained] and associate with them, then you may be sure that the LORD your God will no longer drive out these nations before you."[35] The survival of the nation depended upon Israelites marrying among themselves. Intermarriage with foreign tribes was not an option for those whom God had chosen to represent his character to the nations. Samson's parents knew the rule but had not managed to convey its value to their son.

They now tried to guide Samson toward the desires of God, but they were too late. You can't expect a young man to value the things of God if you don't teach him to value them when he is a boy. Children catch more from you than you deliberately teach them. I value the centering that morning worship with God's people brings to my life not because my parents taught me "good Christian boys go to church" but because they got me out of bed on Sunday morning no matter how late I was out on Saturday night. I saw how our family's song was scored in the key of weekly worship with other families of my faith. I wanted that song in my family's life so we picked up the hymn from my family and sang it in marriage. We continued to sing it, in different keys and variations, for our children, and now they sing a praise chorus of weekly worship for themselves.

But worship is more than "going to church." Rick Warren reminds us that worship is not music and that true worship is a lifestyle.[36] All we do is an act of worship to our Creator. Paul laid the foundation for this concept of worship when he wrote to the ekklesia in Corinth, "So whether you eat or drink or whatever you do, do it all for the glory of God." As Christians mature, they should be able to see that the value of worship clearly is more important than just rote practice.[37] Samson never seemed to grasp the difference.

Samson's parents, after apparently neglecting to instill the lifestyle of worship in their son, tried to use God's words as a triage effort to keep their son from marrying someone they didn't like. Parents misuse God's desires that way, too. "You know God wouldn't be happy with children who do such things," a parent may cry, but unless the children catch the value of godliness, they will not hear the words of their parents. Samson's parents did offer that some relative or some other woman in all of Israel could be as attractive or acceptable as the Philistine girl, but it was too little parenting, too late in a son's life.

Samson would not take no for an answer. Spoiled brats never do. He looked his father in the eye and basically said, "Get her for me. She's the right one for me." No discussion. The child bullied the parent, and he got his way. Samson may have been taller than his father and outweighed him in muscle mass, but children don't always know better than their parents what is best for them. He had no moral or experiential frame of reference for his declaration. How many children have made the same announcement to their parents, received the same advice as Samson, and rejected it—but soon found that Mom and Dad knew what they were talking about? You can see the storm clouds of a bad marriage gathering on the horizon like a cold front moving through North Texas in March. The self-centered strong man was not changing his mind because of his parents' advice. "What did they know?" he smugly asked himself. Samson never learned what Donald Miller confessed, "The most difficult lie I have ever contended with is this: Life is a story about me."[38]

BAD CHOICE, NO PROBLEM

If you are a person of faith, you observe the lives of others with the assumption that God is in control and no matter the circumstances, God will accomplish his purposes. You cling to the promise that "we know that in all things God works for the good of those who love him, who have been called according to his purpose."[39] God is God. Whether Samson makes a hasty choice for his wife, or terrorists fly planes into the World Trade Center towers, or a tornado hits an elementary school on graduation night, God offers redemption so those involved can know God's love and forgiveness in ways they could not have otherwise. Like my friend Mark standing before his burning house, people who trust God is in control can watch what they thought was theirs burn to the ground with the hope that something new will rise in its place.

Samson's storyteller is a person of faith. He adds a parenthetical statement for the reader to remind us not to worry about Samson's choice for a wife. God was aware of Samson's bad parental situation and lustful decision from the beginning. God would handle this. Read with hope the storyteller's words, "His parents did not know that this [decision] was from the Lord, who was seeking an occasion to confront the Philistines; for at that time they were ruling over Israel." Samson's parents knew he made an unwise decision that was outside their good judgment *and* God's commands. God's goal, however, was to push back the Philistines, and if a spoiled, eye-candy-driven young man wanted to marry one of the enemy, then God would get the work done that way. Whether your theological loyalties lie with Arminius or Calvin, you see God's providence at work in the midst of personal choice here.

God's purposes included protection for his people because they were the means of bringing a right relationship with the Lord to the world. As long as the tribes of Israel embodied God's presence among all peoples, God would work through them. When God chose warrior judges to protect his people, God forced himself to work through whatever decisions and character the judge possessed. God gives us all the freedom to choose. Too often, we are more like Samson than like Jesus in our choices, yet God gets his work of redemption done.

Anne Lamott tells of her childhood home—a world saturated with drugs, alcoholism, and ethical ambiguity—in her memoir, *Traveling Mercies*.[40] You could conclude that such a home environment and the choices that flowed from such a situation could not produce a person of faith. Anne confesses that although she could answer the question, "Are you born again?" in the affirmative, her friends saw her as "Christian-ish," like Jonathan Miller said he was not a Jew, but Jew-ish. Somewhere in the middle of a busted-up family and a father's death to cancer, God was present and led her to a leap of faith that landed her story into the lap of thousands who have found hope in her honest confessions.

This paradox of God working through bad choices gives me hope today. Some people think God can use only those who live exactly as God commands and grow up in ideal families. But the truth of His-story is that God works often in the opposite of what we think. God chooses people who can't live up to his standards, who come from broken homes and who aren't the best parents, more often than the ideal citizen with perfect parenting skills. God chose Samson to accomplish his purpose. At this stage of the game, God stayed with his choice no matter whom Samson turned out to be. Covenant love works like that.

"When Jesus saw her . . ."

Dr. Luke tells us a story of Jesus teaching in a synagogue where there was a woman who had been crippled for eighteen years and "could not straighten up at all."[41] Luke tells us, "When Jesus saw her, he called her forward and said to her, 'Woman, you are set free from your infirmity.' Then he put his hands on her, and immediately she straightened up and praised God." When Jesus saw the woman this Savior was attracted to her need, not her beauty. Jesus moved to make her whole, not fill a need for female companionship. Samson saw a woman and had his daddy get her for him. Jesus saw a woman and healed her.

The biblical storytellers do not mention that Jesus considered marriage. He never took a wife or had children. Since it was normal and reasonable that he be married according to the customs of the day, rumors that Jesus took a wife have rustled the leaves of faith since the Age of Reason descended upon history. Don't forget, however, that it was also normal and reasonable that the Messiah of that day have either military or religious backing and that Jesus had neither, and he is still the Messiah. Dan Brown, in his fictional novel, *The Da Vinci Code*, propagated the myth that Jesus married Mary Magdalene and that the Holy Grail is the secret that Jesus had children whose bloodline exists today. Brown popularized the conspiracy theory that the Roman Catholic Church has suppressed the fact of Jesus' marriage and lineage to keep his ancestors from surfacing in order to protect their teachings about Jesus' deity. No credible evidence supports this fanciful notion, but a culture suspicious of religious authority finds it fascinating. Reason has replaced revelation as the primary way of knowing truth. Postmodern epistemology can be summed up in the axiom, "if something is reasonable, it's possible," and some drive over the cliff to conclude, "then it must be true."

Jesus' single devotion to the call of God on his life and his refusal to indulge in the human joy of marriage tells us much about who he was as Savior. Not even the deepest sexual urges he created in human beings could seduce him away from his calling as the Suffering Servant Messiah. His singleness shows his devotion to his calling over his personal wants and needs. Jesus declared, "For I have come down from heaven not to do my will but to do the will of him who sent me."[42] Marriage was not part of the deal any more than a secure career with retirement was part of what the Father sent him to do. Postmodern philosophies find it hard to embrace that kind of commitment.

THE LION

Samson's parents gave in and agreed to go with him to Timnah to see his chosen bride. On the way he separated from his parents. He wandered off like any young man would who scoped the countryside for adventure or just daydreamed about his newfound love. As he approached the outlying vineyards of the town, "suddenly a young lion came roaring toward him." Lions lurked in the vineyards to prey on the easy pickings of those who passed by. It reminds me of the mountain lions of Southern California that find hikers and bikers easier prey than other animals as people push their houses and hobbies farther into the wilderness. We forget, as one park ranger noted in an interview about the rise in killings on the trails, that "When you enter the wilderness you enter the food chain." Samson must have looked like a feast to this young lion.

Our storyteller notes that as the lion lunged toward Samson, the "Spirit of the LORD came upon him in power so that he tore the lion apart with his bare hands as he might have torn a young goat." We will look more deeply into the meaning of the Spirit of the LORD in Samson's life as a savior, but here it points to the fact that the Spirit did not simply "stir him" (Hebrew: pa`am, which means to disturb or impel) as when he was growing up. Now the Spirit came upon him (Hebrew: tsalach, which means to prosper or make successful). It engulfed him, empowered him, and made his physical strength supernatural. He was, in that moment, the warrior God created him to be. The flame of the Spirit dwelled within him as God's way of ensuring his savior could do all he was birthed to accomplish. The power of the Spirit to kill a lion would build confidence for him later when he would face the Philistines.

I remember seeing a guy tear a New York City phone book in half. I was impressed, but I soon learned that a mere mortal like myself could do the same once I learned the secret of breaking the binding and pulling the book apart. I don't believe there is any such secret for tearing a lion apart with your bare hands as you might tear a young goat. I can't find any binding to break on animals, and I can't see how a man can tear apart either a goat or a lion. Samson surely was stronger than any of us can imagine. That's the point of the incident.

The flame of the Spirit empowered God's savior to meet a threat and showed him God's promises were true.

Samson kept his feat hidden from his parents. Samson liked secrets, and we will see how he toyed with others to hide his lies and how he held his greatest secret—the strength that flowed from his hair—as a jeweler holds his most precious diamond, never intending to share it with others so that he could keep it for only himself.

I like Samson as a man *Wild at Heart*. In so many ways he is like William Wallace of Scotland and the fictional character of Maximus Decimus Meridius in *The Gladiator*—all are archetypes of raw masculine strength. Samson could kill an attacking lion with his bare hands and lustfully choose and have the woman of his choice. He was chosen by God and wildly untamed by traditions and mores. He was what legends are made of and what I imagine every man and woman who knew him wanted to become. Compared to our images of Jesus as a man, most people would choose Samson as their savior and hero. Hey, he got all the goods, all the women, and still ended up doing what God wanted him to do.

The irony of it all is that this savior was not sufficient to satisfy a man's deepest longing: a right relationship with his Father in heaven. God used him, and God can use men just like him. We don't need to become less than we are in order for God to use us. But position, power, and prestige are secondary to what's going on in our hearts. In the end, we'll find that the savior who seems the less glamorous of the two truly is our only hope for salvation *because* he completed his God-ordained mission for his life.

This scene of our story ends with the summary statement, "Then he went down and talked with the woman, and he liked her." Samson finally talked with the woman of his desires. He liked her, so his parents returned home to plan a wedding.

Samson killed the lion by strength and spirit. He would not be so successful with the lioness he was about to marry.

DISCUSSION QUESTIONS _____

1. If you are married, describe your feelings when you met your spouse for the first time? If you are single, describe a time you were immediately attracted to someone. How are these feelings helpful in finding the one we will marry? How are they detrimental?

2. How powerful is "the lust of the eyes" in your life? How do your eyes serve you? How do they draw you away from the purposes of God for your life?

3. How did your parents mold your character growing up? How did they teach you to trust God; through keeping rules and doing the right things? Or did they spend more time guiding you to have a relationship with God? If you have children, how do you mold their character and faith?

4. What decisions did you make growing up that were counter to your parents' advice and your parents' advice turned out to be right?

5. How has God accomplished his purposes in your life even when you have made bad choices? Or are you willing to accept that biblical perspective on how God works in our choices?

Chapter Six

THE RIDDLE

Out of the eater, something to eat;
Out of the strong, something sweet.

— JUDGES 14:14

"What's black and white and red all over?" I asked my third grade buddy.

"I don't know. What?" he replied, playing the straight man.

"A newspaper," I declared with a smile.

My friend moaned. He knew the punch line would be something silly like that. We shared the same stock jokes at that age. Passed from older children to younger, these riddles represented a stage of understanding for boys and girls. To tell the same riddles seriously in the tenth grade would tell your peers that despite being their age, you were nowhere near their maturity.

More serious riddles replace childhood ones as we grew up. "Knock-knock" jokes are replaced by questions like "Why do bad things happen to good people?" "I prayed like Jesus said for her to be healed, and she died anyway. Why?" "Why war?" or, "I prayed the *Prayer of Jabez*, and I'm still driving a Civic. What's up with that?" As children, we eventually knew all the answers to our classmates' riddles. Becoming an adult means you learn the riddles but never fully know the answers.

A Riddle of Life

I traveled to Albania once to take a look at the mission work we had supported for seven years. We met our contact in Tirana, the capital, and made our way to where she lived in Shkoder. She took us to an orphanage where she had worked during her early days in the country. Parents who left their homeland for work or those who had walked away from their children because they could not feed them anymore had abandoned thousands of them. The worker told stories of girls forced to leave the state-run orphanages at age sixteen only to be taken by the mafia and forced into worldwide prostitution rings. As I looked into the eyes of the little girls, I was haunted by the riddle, "What if my two daughters had been born here instead of the U.S.? What would their lives look like at eighteen and twenty-one?" I had no answer to that riddle.

Later, we made our way to the region of Trapoje and the town of Friese in Zone B, a town created by the former dictator Enver Hoxha to house workers. The apartment complexes were traditional, communist block, cement structures that had become homes for people trying to survive after the country's economy crashed in the early nineties. Most of the inhabitants had moved from mountain villages where they had farmed to town, seeking jobs that did not exist. Sadness hovered over the community like mist over the coast of Wales—except in one apartment. In this two-room sanctuary, a small group of young followers of Jesus gathered weekly to worship, teach the Bible, and enjoy the fellowship of other followers. I sensed I was seeing the *ekklesia* as Paul longed for it to be.

Teenage Christians taught preschoolers Bible stories in what was formerly a kitchen. The elementary-aged children huddled in the adjoining room. They sang songs about Jesus and God's love. After the children's lessons about thirty young adults gathered to sing praises to God and hear the witness of the Word in a fourteen- by fourteen-foot room. Their praises bounced off the concrete walls and floated out the windows into the streets of the town where they mingled with the shouts and cheers of a soccer game being played in the town's only field.

As I observed the Christ worshippers in that tiny apartment and knew of their intelligence, ingenuity, strength of soul, and desire to follow Jesus, I wondered what would have happened to this group of people if they'd all been born in America. Riddles broke into my thoughts like a commercial into my favorite episode of *24*. I wondered, would their passion and desire for God be as great? Would there even be a group of disciples with whom they would *want* to participate? Would they be as involved in their community? What ministry would the brother and sister who translated for us find if they had been born in Dallas? Would the seven sisters who wove carpets on a homemade loom start their own business, or would they never have learned the art of weaving because they played video games and watched television all night? What if they lived in a prosperous country where 60 percent were of their same faith and not of another? What if they had grown up in a "Christian country" rather than in an atheistic, communist country thrown into chaos by freedom?

These were riddles to which I would never learn the answers, but the puzzles challenged my faith and caused me to sit humbly before God.

Stolen Honey and Hired Companions

Samson loved riddles—questions to trick and win advantage over others. On his return trip to Timnah to marry his bride, Samson came across the lion he had killed earlier. In the carcass was "a swarm of bees and some honey." Most of us would take a look at such a sight from a distance, but not Samson. He realized his strength and indestructibility. He was afraid of nothing and no one. He dipped his hand into the hive's harvest, and tasted it. He liked what he ate and later gave some to his parents who traveled with him.

Samson's self-service approach to the lion reveals another weakness of our hero's character. As a Nazirite, he was not to touch the body of a dead animal. This was a core command of the angel to God's messenger. For that matter, any good Jew who touched a dead creature would become "unclean" and unfit to participate in the rituals of worship to the Lord. As with his rebellion in choosing a non-Jewish wife, Samson picked and chose which rules he would follow and defy. His lack of discipline and pride resulted in an arrogance that led him to disobey God's guidelines for living and to create his own.

When Samson brought the honey to his parents, he did not tell them where he had found it. If he had told them the truth, they might have protested and lectured him about touching a dead thing. He wanted none of that. On the other hand, given their passiveness about earlier decisions, they may have simply looked at each other like parents in Wal-Mart next to their temper-tantrum-throwing child with the look that asks, "Are you going to take care of this or do I have to?" The father takes the easy way out, gives the child the toy he is screaming about, and they leave the scene of the disturbance as quickly as possible. There comes a time in parenting that if you didn't do your job in the child's formative years, you simply turn your head in the adult years. This is how dysfunction perpetuates itself from generation to generation.

When the family arrived in town, Samson's father went to the woman's house and finalized the wedding plans. Our storyteller relates, "And Samson made a feast there, as was customary for bridegrooms." In this passage, we get another clue about Samson's life. The writer notes, "When he [Samson] appeared, he was given thirty companions." Most men have their friends join them when they marry. Samson "was given" his companions.

My wife, being a people person, wanted as many friends as possible to be part of our wedding party. She asked eight friends to be her bridesmaids. Yes, eight. Which meant I had to ask eight of my friends to be groomsmen. Kim's problem was whittling down her list to so few! Even though the four years before our wedding had been filled with meaningful, life-deepening friendships, finding that many friends who would travel to Dallas, hang out with me for the weekend, and get dressed up in pastel-colored tuxedo shirts was a little harder for me. But real friends do that kind of thing—even if it means wearing a pink tux shirt with ruffles. Thanks, guys.

It's odd to me that Samson "was given thirty companions." Companions are not like friends. You are my companion when we travel together to present a seminar to a group of people in another town. You are my friend when I choose to call you to run on a beautiful spring day or to talk over a cup of coffee. Granted, Samson was not in his hometown, but friends travel to friends' weddings. Samson's father, it seems, had to get stand-ins for Samson.

If you read ahead in our story, you will discover Samson always was alone—except when he was with women who were usually trying to seduce his secrets from him. He lived alone, fought alone, and loved alone. No one stood by him at his death. Co-opted companions at his marriage foreshadowed the life of loneliness he was to live. David had Jonathan. Naomi had Ruth. Samson had rented companions.

Jesus and His Friends

One of the turning points in Jesus' relationship with his disciples was when he told them they were no longer like servants doing what they were commanded to do. They had become his friends. By this time, this band of people had shared the highs and lows of life together. They had been part of the feeding of five thousand plus people with only the contents of a boy's lunch. They had seen the blind and lame healed. They had huddled in the wilderness regions waiting for Jesus to finish praying. They had been tossed like a toy boat in a bathtub on the Sea of Galilee and had seen Peter stumble toward Jesus as he walked on water. They shared food, ridicule, and acceptance. Jesus brought them together on mission, but he had also nurtured them into a community.

Toward the end of his public ministry Jesus told his companions, "Greater love has no one than this, that he lay down his life for his friends."[43] And then he added, "You are my friends if you do what I command you to do." Jesus did not state the obvious and then gather the guys around for a group hug. He defined friendship among his followers by their actions: a friend to Jesus is someone who does what he asked them to do. A true friend will come over in the middle of the night to sit with you or spend a day off helping you move from one apartment to another. You can call friends without feeling guilty or worrying that they wish they had never met you.

"A friend loves at all times"[44] was one of the first verses from the Bible I learned as a child. I still hold to that truth, but I've learned that while you can share ministry with others, until you share the ups and downs of life with them, they cannot become friends. When those bonds are built, separating can be hard. My deepest hurts have come from those who called me friend, yet seemed to walk away easily. They leave with the line, "We'll still be friends," a groundless promise that feels like a seventh grade breakup. Those words only placate the one walking away and do nothing for the one left behind. As a pastor, I've found that some of my most painful losses have been those with whom I've shared ministry, only to have them leave the congregation in which we'd all worked so hard.

But Jesus doesn't leave—he taught that "a good shepherd lays down his life for the sheep,"[45] and he demonstrated his belief in those words when he died on the cross. Jesus was a friend and had friends, those for whom he died. He also knew what it meant for friends to walk away in tough times, even to betray him. He knew what King David, his spiritual forefather, recorded in his journal of psalms:

If an enemy were insulting me,
I could endure it;
if a foe were raising himself against me,
I could hide from him.
But it is you, a man like myself,
my companion, my close friend,
with whom I once enjoyed sweet fellowship
as we walked with the throng at the house of God.[46]

David knew the sting of one close to him choosing to turn his back on him and to leave him standing alone with all the responsibility of leading. Some believe David spoke of Ahithophel, "the king's counselor."[47] Ahithophel was among the conspirators with David's son, Absalom, who tried to overthrow the king.[48] "But it is you" rings like "*et tu Brute!*" in the ears of those who look into the eyes of their betrayers.

Jesus endured Judas's betrayal, but Peter's denial had to pile on the pain. Jesus suffered physically during his Passion and death, but his spiritual lashes came from the desertions of Peter and the other disciples. Only the unnamed "one whom Jesus loved"[49] made it to the foot of the cross.

I am sometimes surprised who ends up standing with me during the toughest times. The Peters who loudly announce their loyalty often fall in the fray, or they wait until the battles are over, then walk away. Yet, there always seems to be someone who pushes through the struggle and stands by me even at my demise, because we have loved each other, while others have been only my companions. All of us survive life's betrayals because God graces us with friends who walk through our pain with us. These friendships keep us from becoming cynical, despite the betrayal of others.

You can work with someone and never become friends, but when people share the same passion for the same mission, mountain-moving friendships result. Jesus knew this and invested his life in making friends who would lay down their lives for each other. He risked the pain of friendship to ensure others would know the love of God firsthand.

Samson seems to have never connected with anyone as a friend. He was strong and handsome, but as far as we know, he lived and died alone. The advantage of his solitary lifestyle was that, at his death, he did not carry the weight of deserting friends to his grave. But I'm not sure which is more painful: dying while friends turn their backs on you or dying with not one friend to witness your death. While Jesus may have borne more pain, he also touched more lives. I'll continue to risk the pain of friendship.

The Riddle

Since Samson's wedding companions were not friends, and perhaps because they were not Israelites, he apparently felt free to turn his intelligence to trickery. He made a deal with his newly gathered companions:

> Let me tell you a riddle. If you can give me the answer within the seven days of the feast, I will give you thirty linen garments and thirty sets of clothes. If you can't tell me the answer, you must give me thirty linen garments and thirty sets of clothes.

Samson had a secret. He had touched a dead animal, and he still had his strength. He had rebelled against God's ways, and he could have risen up and killed another lion if he had wanted. Pride-filled people can't keep secrets to themselves. For others to know about their rebellion and seemingly victorious living in spite of their disobedience only adds to their self-perceived legends. I imagine Samson felt he had to tell, but he could not confess the truth outright, so he twisted his secret into a riddle to benefit his growing ego. His companions took the bait and asked for the riddle. Samson gave it to them:

> Out of the eater, something to eat;
> Out of the strong, something sweet.

Since we have read about Samson taking honey from the carcass of a lion, we know the answer, but even so, I have to admit Samson was clever. He created an excellent riddle; his intelligence and wit combined to confound his enemies. In seven days, he would have thirty new linen garments to strut in front of his new wife. So he thought. King Solomon knew better when he wrote, "Pride goes before destruction, and haughtiness before a fall."[50]

Jesus' Riddles

Jesus told riddles, too. His were more stories than snares, and with his parables, he built up people and gave insight into the things of God. For example, he told a riddle to a Pharisee who had invited him over to his house for a meal. This was the time a "sinful woman" washed Jesus' feet with her tears and wiped them with her hair. She also poured expensive perfume on his feet between sobs. When the religious host questioned what she was doing, Jesus told this riddle:

> Two men owed money to a certain moneylender. One owed him five hundred denarii, and the other fifty. Neither of them had the money to pay him back, so he canceled the debts of both. Now which of them will love him more?[51]

The Pharisee got the answer but missed the truth. Of course, the guy who owed more was most grateful. Jesus used the riddle to teach that the woman was the more gracious host, and that the religious leader had acted more like the less-forgiven debtor.

Jesus told riddles about the kingdom of God. Jesus chose stories over syllogisms and mystery over precepts to relay God's truth to all of us. He said the kingdom of God was like a lost sheep found by its shepherd, a lost coin found after its owner turned the house upside down, and a lost son who returned home to the open arms of his father.[52] Jesus spoke in riddles about mustard seeds, yeast, pearls, and hidden treasures.[53] Matthew tells us "Jesus spoke all these things to the crowd in parables; he did not say anything to them without using a parable." Why did he teach that way? "So was fulfilled what was spoken through the prophet: I will open my mouth in parables, I will utter things hidden since the creation of the world."[54] He told his riddles, or parables, stories, and metaphors, in order to help people know God and to reveal the deeper things of life.

Jesus also told riddles like "Blessed are the poor in spirit, for theirs is the kingdom of heaven," or, "Blessed are the meek, for they will inherit the earth."[55] His brainteasers challenged how people saw life but gave to every hurting person what he or she needed to hear. Jesus did not tell riddles to maliciously trick others or to extract gain for himself. His stories were simple and timeless because he wanted everyone to understand what he was saying. He knew their lives depended on it.

Our hero Jesus used his intelligence and wit in the service of God and for all people. Our hero Samson used those gifts for his own advantage. Once again, it comes down to the question of whom do you serve: God or ego?

Solving the Puzzle

By the fourth day, Samson's hired companions became frustrated. They could not decipher the foreigner's secret. Samson's pride must have grown in proportion with their anxiety. But the companions did what many who have to win to avoid paying off a bet would do—they bullied someone who could get the information for them. They were at the feast because they were paid to befriend the groom of a family friend, not to be taken by a foreigner. They pulled Samson's wife aside one day and threatened her, "Coax your husband into explaining the riddle for us, or we will burn you and your father's household to death. Did you invite us here to rob us?"

Samson's bride was in a tight spot. Her family had prepared for the wedding. Friends had left their fields for the feast, and now guys she may have known since childhood were about to be taken for a camel-load of clothing by a stranger whose ancestors were sheep-herding invaders. Blood *is* thicker than arranged weddings. Loyalties are tested when your life is on the line. She hurled all her charm into finding the riddle's answer. A dreadful husband-wife clash followed.

She began by throwing herself on him and sobbing. This tactic was followed by the laser-guided smart bomb, "You hate me!"

"Where did that come from?" I imagine Samson wondering. He loved the crying woman in his arms, but now she was saying, "You hate me?" He may have asked himself, "What did I say at lunch?" before starting through his file of "things that might have upset my wife."

She continued to sob, "You don't really love me. You've given my people a riddle, but you haven't told me the answer." In my opinion, "You don't love me" is an arrow to a man's heart. That comment cuts to the core of a man: he provides because he loves his wife; he protects because he loves her; he works long hours because he loves her. Accusing a man of not loving his wife bends his mind like an eighteen-wheeler jackknifed on black ice between Pueblo and Colorado Springs.

Samson countered her expressed insecurities with the excuse, "I haven't even explained it to my father or mother, so why should I explain it to you?" Jesus said, "A man should leave his mother and father and cling to his wife so the two can become one flesh."[56] Samson had not left his mother and father in the sense that telling them a secret trumped telling his wife-to-be the secret. Any seasoned spouse could see where this was headed: Samson was now trapped. And his wife knew it.

We are told that "she cried the whole seven days of the feast," which surely got in the way of honeymoon activities. Finally, on the seventh day, the day the local boys had to have the answer, Samson told her "because she continued to press him." Even with all his strength, Samson couldn't hold out against his wailing bride for seven days. Before the day was over, the men of the town answered him with Jeopardy-like questions:

What is sweeter than honey?
What is stronger than a lion?

Samson must have turned red-faced and come out of his chair. His smug demeanor changed to that of the roaring lion that started this whole thing. He spoke again in not-so-cryptic code,

"If you had not plowed with my heifer, you would not have solved my riddle."

That pretty much ended the marriage right there. Samson roared his true feelings about his wife, the heifer. His pride-filled plan had failed. Now he was on the hook for the goods, and his pride would not stand for this.

Samson's riddle at his wedding showed his wit and intelligence, qualities of any good leader. Yet those traits mounted on an empty heart will be set aside eventually for brute strength to get the job done. Compromise and negotiations are not options for a wounded ego. Samson was about to show how strong he really was to those who had beat him at his own game.

DISCUSSION QUESTIONS

1. What were some of your favorite childhood riddles? What riddles of life do you now know but have no concrete answers for?

2. What experiences have shown you that people who have had a different life situation than you may have an advantage in their relationship with God simply because their social, religious, or economic environment is different than yours?

3. Who has been like Jesus to you in a friendship? Peter? Judas? How has that friendship affected how you enter into other friendships?

4. Which of Jesus' stories or "riddles" do you like the most? Which ones help you understand the ways and person of God most?

5. How do you evaluate Samson's wife's tactic to get the answer from him? Given her circumstances was she justified? Are there other reasons why Samson gave in other than he was tired of her whining? What would you have done?

Chapter Seven

REVENGE

This time I have a right to get even with the Philistines;
I will really harm them . . .

—JUDGES 15:3

I n the summer before my ninth grade year in high school, I went up to the school gym to play basketball with friends. We were shooting around when a guy two years older than me began to shoot at the other end of the court. He was the school's stud athlete and was to begin his junior year in the fall. One of my friends dared me to throw a basketball and hit him. Hey, we were soon-to-be-ninth graders on summer break. Of course, I took the dare. I had to prove I was worthy of walking the same halls with that guy once school started. I launched the ball, and much to my horror, it arched perfectly and hit him square in the back of the head. Everyone froze. A lone ball bounced on the hardwood floor. Like Wyatt Erp challenged to a gunfight, he turned around and asked, "Who did that?" My friends all pointed to me and scattered. He started toward me in a full sprint, and I could tell he was about to prove I was *not* worthy to walk in his high school halls. My normal modus operandi in matters such as this is to launch a humorous anecdote and begin negotiations. My pursuer's eyes, however, said diplomacy was not an option, so I chose my second most effective method of encountering trouble that I had stirred up. I ran.

He pursued me around the outside of the gym and around the school for some time, but his speed and strength gained on me with every step. As we circled the gym and re-entered the door we had exited, I was getting winded and he was getting madder. I stopped, and turned to face him. When I did, he hit me in the face with a swing that had been building momentum since he had begun the chase. I fell back onto the floor and grabbed my nose. I know my eyes were the size of a guy who had just completed his first X Games-type jump on his skateboard and was lying at the bottom of the stairs wondering if anything was broken after the fall. My pursuer took another step toward me. I was doomed. He glared at me like Shaq O'Neal after he had slam dunked over Yao Ming, when Ming laid full-length on his back under the basket. He paused. He stared into my watering eyes. Then he stepped over me, and walked to the dressing room. He remained the alpha dog, and I, the younger, weaker challenger.

I never randomly challenged an upper classmate again. My broken nose was a daily reminder of how overt challenges to those more powerful can end. Natural instinct always leads to revenge. That's the way we are wired. Fight or flight, and all that. Only a force outside us can restrain us from first strike options and keep us from acting out our anger toward those we believe have hurt us.

Our next scenes in Samson's story tell of his revenge toward those whom he perceived had wronged him. Revenge flows out of an instinctive need to have our way and builds on ego's insistence to be right. We often pervert justice into revenge, but they are not the same. Some quote the earliest Judaic code of "Show no pity: life for life, eye for eye, tooth for tooth, hand for hand, foot for foot"[57] as God's support of revenge in human relationships. World powers exchange nuclear threats and suicide bombers in carrying out this philosophy of vengeance. Samson called on the practice when his hired friends solved his riddle. He wanted revenge for his hurt ego.

THE SPIRIT OF THE LORD

An interesting twist to the riddle story follows after Samson's hired friends broke the wedding code. We are told, "Then the Spirit of the Lord came upon him in power." This is the third of four uses of this phrase in our tale. The first was when the writer told of Samson growing up as a child. The second use was when he tore the lion apart, and the fourth and last time was when he broke out of the ropes that bound him and he killed a thousand of his enemies with the drying jawbone of a donkey. This phrase vividly depicts God's presence in Samson's life as a spiritual steroid that peaked his physical strength and turned him into a superhero. The Spirit of the Lord soared in the flame of Samson's power.

The phrase "the Spirit of the Lord" is not uncommon in our book of heroes. Othniel, Israel's first judge, received the Spirit of the Lord as he went into war.[58] The same Spirit came upon Gideon as he took his place of leadership and summoned the tribes of Israel to war against "the Midianites, Amalekites and other eastern peoples."[59] The same was true of Jephthah when he mustered an army against the Ammonites.[60] The only other use of the phrase in the record of Judges is with our savior, Samson. The writer used the phrase to acknowledge God's empowerment of his chosen leader. It is another way to remind the reader that victory did not come by human strength and leadership but by the power of God in a person's life.

The story tells of an apparent progression of effect when "the Spirit of the Lord" came upon Samson. He killed a single lion, followed by the death of thirty men, then the destruction of a thousand men in less time than it takes to assemble an army that size. I wonder what the extent of his deliverance of Israel would have been in the power of the Spirit of the Lord if he had not met Delilah? I also wonder why the writer did not use the phrase when Samson pulled the temple of Dagon down upon the worshippers on the day of his death? And I wonder how much more God could have empowered Samson if he had not let his ego drive his use of God's strength in his life?

JESUS AND THE SPIRIT

When Jesus came out of the water after his baptism by John, the chronicler tells us, "At that moment heaven was opened, and he saw the Spirit of God descending like a dove and lighting on him."[61] We are also told a voice was heard from the heavens saying, "This is my Son, whom I love; with him I am well pleased." God the Father blessed the Son as he stepped out of the river and into the stream of God's purposes for redemption. Some suggest that Joseph had not given the paternal blessing, "This is my son, whom I love; with whom I am well pleased," because after the angel visits and events surrounding Jesus' birth, he could never bring himself to call Jesus his son. If no blessing came at the boy's bar mitzvah, then this was Jesus' true Father's blessing of his Son. The flame of God's Spirit hovered over the Sent One, to show where his power would come from.

Rather than tearing up a lion or killing his enemies after his baptism experience, Jesus followed the Spirit into the wilderness to be tested. Maybe Samson would have been more effective if he had followed the same path—testing before a tirade could materialize. Maybe he would not have used his Spirit-filled strength for revenge. Maybe he would have used his spiritual power for healing rather than for destruction.

Pay Off and Pay Back

Samson owed his wedding party thirty new sets of clothes. But he had been betrayed, and in his egocentric way of thinking, he owed them nothing. They cheated. So he went to the nearest town and killed thirty men, stripped them of their clothes, returned to his so-called friends, and stacked the bloodstained clothes in front of them. Like a child who cleans his room with a scowl on his face, Samson fulfilled his obligation. He paid for the bet he lost. "Burning with anger" at what they had done to him, he returned to his father's house.

Anger motivated his actions. The process is universal. When my ego is wounded and I mull over that wrong, anger builds. Soon, I am either plotting the ruin or hurt of the one who wounded me, or I am attacking him to let him know what he had done to me. Pride is the source of anger, just as brokenness is the source of compassion.

It doesn't take much to start the nuclear reaction that can cause a relational Chernobyl. Some time after the wedding riddle incident, "at the time of the wheat harvest," Samson decided to make a visit to his abandoned wife. He took along a goat as a gift and insisted he go into her room when he arrived. Her father met Samson at the door and said that he had given her to one of Samson's purchased friends since he was convinced Samson hated her for her betrayal. To reduce the offense, the father offered his younger daughter to Samson as a substitute bride. Perhaps we should write "pregnant pause" in the margin of the script here. If you were watching an old western, you would hear ominous music playing in the background as our hero squinted into the sun and shifted his cigar to the other side of his mouth. Tumbleweeds would roll down Main Street. You know what would happen next. That's why you pay for a ticket to see the film.

Samson reasoned like many of us do when we have not let go of an offense, saying "This time I have a right to get even with the Philistines; I will really harm them." At least with the riddle, the men had clearly won, if by unfair means, but now he had a real reason to inflict some pain on his enemies. Who would argue that a man whose father-in-law had given his wife to another man did not have a *right* to do something about such an offense? Samson seems to have believed he had justified grounds for mass destruction. One person among the Philistines had hurt him, so why not spread the payback as far through those people as possible?

Revenge, unlike *agape* love, keeps a record of wrongs, and when the balance sheet leans toward retribution action is required. Samson devised a never-used-before war machine—bionic flamethrowers! Our storyteller describes his work:

So he went out and caught three hundred foxes and tied them tail to tail in pairs. He then fastened a torch to every pair of tails, lit the torches and let the foxes loose in the standing grain of the Philistines.[62]

I have to admire Samson's ingenuity and skill. Catching three hundred foxes (or jackals, depending on your translation), corralling them long enough to tie two tails together with a burning torch, and releasing them into wheat fields took more-than-human strength, intelligence, and agility. Samson was a remarkable specimen.

The results were on the scale of Samson's superhuman desire for revenge. The Bible records that the fire consumed "the shocks and standing grain, together with the vineyards and olive groves," a catastrophic blow to the Philistine econ-omy. This new kind of fox-fire destroyed both the gathered grain and the stand-ing grain in the fields. It spread like a West Texas wind over drought-conditioned grasslands into the vineyards and olive groves. Samson had to be proud of his work. He must have smiled as the fields burned and he watched the people try to put out the fires. He surely chuckled as the foxes tried to get apart from each other while the fire climbed up their tails. Chaos danced over the countryside.

One act of revenge, however, *always* leads to another. An eye for an eye ultimately ends in blindness for everyone unless someone stops the cycle. Read the newspapers about Palestinian and Jewish reprises when one offends the other over land in the Gaza Strip. Little has changed since Samson fought the Philistines. No one stepped in to stop the dance of revenge in our story. The Philistines, now seriously wounded, exercised *their* right to retaliate. They started by tracking down the family who lit Samson's fire and burned Samson's wife and her father to death.

The payback dance continued. Samson stepped back on the dance floor because the Philistines had murdered the wife he didn't love and the family whom he loathed. The music of vengeance makes us do crazy things. He finally admitted his true motive, "Since you've acted like this, I won't stop until I get my revenge on you." There. He said it. Revenge was why he acted like he did, and in his childish thinking, he found a reason to stay engaged in the battle with his enemies. Right foot, left foot, step slide step. The music of conflict continued.

Our storyteller summarized his actions: "He attacked them viciously and slaughtered many of them." The King James Version records Samson's response this way: "And he smote them hip and thigh with a great slaughter." I'm not sure what "smote them hip and thigh" means, but if he tore them apart like he did the lion on the way to his wedding, then some hips and thighs would have flown over the battlefield.

Jesus on Revenge

Revenge, no matter the injustice, is not in the repertoire of those who follow Jesus. Jesus challenged our natural justification to make things right by matching injustice with revenge when he taught in his inaugural message:

You have heard that it was said, "Eye for eye, and tooth for tooth." But I tell you, Do not resist an evil person. If someone strikes you on the right cheek, turn to him the other also. And if someone wants to sue you and take your tunic, let him have your cloak as well. If someone forces you to go one mile, go with him two miles. Give to the one who asks you, and do not turn away from the one who wants to borrow from you.[63]

Jesus taught that revenge is never a motive for action among those who call him leader. He stops the music of taking up for your wounded ego and teaches a new song of strength. Revenge is easy. It's instinctive. Anyone can fall into it. Love, on the other hand, cuts across your instincts and gives us Samson-like strength to take the blow, give up our cloak, go a second mile, and give to those who ask or want to borrow from us.

Jesus never sought revenge against those who attacked him. During his mockery of a trial that led to his death, he did nothing when his accusers spit in his face and hit him[64]—things Samson would never tolerate peacefully. When Pilate reminded Jesus of the charges the religious leaders brought against him, Jesus made no reply, no here's-why-they-are-wrong speech or defense of his goodness. Jesus already had crucified his ego to the will of his Father. Only the death of his body remained.

The differences between Samson's and Jesus' responses to offense are the differences between our natural responses to those who hurt us and the responses we will show if Jesus truly rules in our hearts.

One Thousand Dead

After Samson delivered this blow to the Philistines, he went to rest in a cave in Etam not far from his home in Zorah. Like Jacob's brother, Esau, Samson preferred nature's housing to the tents of his people. He was a loner and liked living and fighting alone. While he rested from his battle, the Philistines—now burning hotter with anger than their fields and vineyards—crossed over into Judah's territory and set up camp across a region called Lehi, which means "jawbone." Prophetic, wouldn't you say?

When the Judeans asked why the Philistines had shown up uninvited on Israel's side of the fence, they answered, "We have come to take Samson prisoner . . . to do to him as he did to us." Revenge music. At least they sought to kill only the perpetrator, not his entire country—unless, of course, the country did not give up the person behind their pain. After all, they did bring a sizeable army. Power speaks loudest in disputes over who wronged whom the most. Strange that the Philistines showed more restraint in this matter than God's chosen leader. Samson went straight from his wife's family to the fields of their nation rather than punishing just those who had hurt him.

It's possible that Israel knew of Samson and his tirades by now. Perhaps they were secretly happy for his exploits against their enemies, but now the enemy was in their backyard. Samson had become more a hassle than a hero. He had become a threat to their safety. So three thousand Israelites left their harvest fields, mustered an army to match the Philistines, and went down to where Samson stayed. Like parents leaving work to meet with the principal because Junior set off a firecracker in his archrival's locker, they trudged through the sands to restore peace. When they found him they asked, "Don't you realize that the Philistines are rulers over us? What have you done to us?" Or, don't you get that you have angered the people who can destroy us? What were you thinking? But they were not there to fight with Samson; they were there to give him over to those who had set up camp in their backyard.

Samson's answer was in line with his immature behavior, "I merely did to them what they did to me." In other words, "They started it." The Israelites refused his explanation, and said, "We've come to tie you up and hand you over to the Philistines." They were sending the message to the Philistines that they wanted nothing of the battle between Samson and those whose fields were burned. They would hand over their kinsman and get back to their fields for harvest. Food for their families was more important than national honor at this time, and they decided that Samson could fend for himself. The three-thousand-member army helped to ensure the battle stayed between their judge and their enemies. Israel had accepted Philistine dominance and its people were happy to live in submission to them as long as they were left alone. Samson caused the status quo to teeter, and they had to give him to their enemies to restore tolerance.

Samson, I'm not surprised to find, did not see things that way. He made his tribesmen swear they would not kill him themselves, and they agreed. Still, our storyteller notes that they tied him up with "two new ropes," implying that the ropes were particularly strong. This detail sets up the magnitude of our hero's next feat of strength. Samson's captors led him out of the cave and toward the assembled Philistines. When they saw him approaching, they began to shout in pleasure. They were about to get their revenge without a war.

For the fourth time we are told, "The Spirit of the Lord came upon him in power."[65] Samson was about to be the deliverer God created him to become. He was born to push back Israel's enemies, and the Spirit's empowerment demonstrated that. God empowers those he calls when they encounter the very things he called them to do. Samson busted out of the new ropes like they were "charred flax," and he was free. He picked up a jawbone of a donkey, which was still "fresh," moist, and strong. He went to work on the Philistines. Samson, a poet warrior, composed a not-so-polite Hebrew poem as he destroyed his enemies. Here's my translation:

With the jawbone of an ass
I have made asses of them.
With the jawbone of an ass
I have killed a thousand asses.

His countrymen must have stood in amazement, and when he tossed the bloodstained jawbone to the ground, they named the spot *Jawbone Hill*, literally, "the height of the jawbone." Like Bunker Hill in Boston where the outnumbered patriots fought off the English army, Israel memorialized the spot for the God-sized victory Samson won that day.

Samson had his revenge, and in the middle of that self-protective act, God's plan was accomplished. God used Samson to "begin the deliverance of

Israel from the hands of the Philistines" just as the angel had promised at the announcement of this savior's birth. Destroying the Philistine crops and killing thousands of their warriors was part of God's purpose for Samson's birth: as we will see in the story to follow, he held off Israel's enemies for twenty years. Yet Samson's life was about to take a turn that would lead to his downfall.

LEADERSHIP LESSONS

Before we leave this episode in Samson's life we can glean two leadership lessons from his encounter with his enemies. The first is: never lead alone. Leaders unchecked by advisors can wreak havoc among those they lead. Samson's warring was about personal interest, not that of his country. Yes, the country's enemies suffered losses as Samson led, but no one was engaged in his mission. No one shared his advantages of strength and agility.

Solomon, Israel's king who actually led Israel, penned these proverbs for leaders: "Pride only breeds quarrels, but wisdom is found in those who take advice."[66] It appears that Solomon had studied his predecessor's war record: "Make plans by seeking advice; if you wage war, obtain guidance."[67] If Solomon had read Samson's press clippings, he could have seen the greater victories Samson could have achieved with some advice from others. What could have happened if Samson had inspired the three thousand Israelites who came to hand him over to join him rather than see them as an audience for his theater of strength?

When you compare the final results of both leaders, you must take Solomon's advice and seek input from others. Jesus sought advice throughout his ministry from the One who led him, his Father in heaven. Prayer was the heart of his relationship with the Father. He spent nights in prayer and climbed out of the valley of ministry to seek the guidance of the One who sent him.

The second leadership lesson we learn from Samson's exploits is that if displays of strength are the leader's modus operandi for leading, one feat of strength must exceed the previous one to stay in power. Pride is a thirsty partner, and its accomplishments are the sports drink of those who compete in the arena of recognition. After Samson tore the lion, he killed the thirty, which led to capturing and releasing three hundred foxes, and the death of a thousand others. His resumé grew with his pride.

Results are the residue of leadership. Leaders mobilize for change, organize for effectiveness, and inspire for victory. However, the outcomes produced by the leader are most effective when they serve the group or organization, not the leader. Leaders get lost in why they do what they do when their focus turns from building the organization to building their personal reputations.

Jesus did not stack miracle upon miracle for personal gain. After the feeding of the five thousand, for example, rather than heading to the awards banquet to receive a most-people-fed-with-the-least-amount-of-food trophy by a local relief organization, he withdrew to a mountain to pray alone.[68] For Jesus, the purpose of any extraordinary act was to point to God the Father and to give credit where credit was due, not to gain acceptance and power among his peers.

Most leaders produce results, but those results should benefit those they lead. Self-sacrifice is the heart of a servant leader.

Revenge is a powerful motivator. Samson used it effectively to sooth his injured pride. He caused great harm to the enemies of Israel, but he led no one. It was all about him, and his ego-stroking drive would become his Achilles' heel.

This chapter of Samson's life, found in Judges 16, closes by announcing, "Samson led Israel for twenty years in the days of the Philistines." We know the length of his reign but little about the details, and the limited information leads me to believe Samson did nothing extraordinary as a leader.

Discussion Questions _____

1. Did you have a similar experience to the author's high school basketball story he told at the beginning of this chapter? Do you naturally challenge others or are you more passive?

2. What are your answers to the author's proposed questions at the end of the section "The Spirit of the Lord?" (p. 77). What other questions do you have about Samson's life if he had lived a life in the Spirit of the Lord?

3. How has revenge affected your life? Have you been the recipient of it—justified or not? Have you ever justified your actions toward another on the basis of revenge?

4. How do you respond to Jesus' teaching on revenge from the Sermon on the Mount? Have you ever practiced "turning the other cheek" rather than taking an "eye for an eye?" What are some of the practical difficulties of living this way?

5. The author describes two "leadership lessons" from the incident between Samson and the Philistines. How do you respond to these two lessons?

Chapter Eight

MEET MY NEEDS, OH GOD!

Must I now die of thirst and
fall into the hands of the uncircumcised?

—JUDGES 15:18

You can tell a man's character by two things: how he prays and how he manages his sex drive. How a man prays exposes his heart and to whom he bends his knee. How he manages his sexual urges exposes the depth of discipline in his life. Hypocrisy can mask both aspects of his life, and he can act out a persona many will accept as real. However, crisis and leisure are crucibles that reveal a person's true character. No Oscar-winning performance can hide a man's true identity in the heat of crisis or in the calm of leisure.

Our storyteller records only two prayers of Samson: the first after he killed the thousand Philistines with the jawbone, the second just before his death. We will save the second prayer for when we observe Samson's demise, but we can note here that in both cases, Samson asked God to serve him, rather than the other way around. The warrior-judge cried out to God after his victory over his enemies. He was thirsty and his lips were parched. He prayed,

"You have given your servant this great victory. Must I now die of thirst and fall into the hands of the uncircumcised?"

Samson was in crisis. He had depleted his body's fluids, and he was near death by dehydration. He must have felt like Aron Ralston on his sixth day of his hand trapped under a rock in the Blue John Canyon near Moab, Utah. He craved water after his supply had run out and he had turned to drinking his urine to survive. While as far as we know, Ralston prayed no such prayer before he cut off his hand to free himself, Samson cried out desperately to God for rescue from the bind he was in.

Samson acknowledged that God had given the victory in his prayer. This is the only instance of such a confession by the strong man. In his other exploits, he neglects giving credit to God. I guess he thought in every other incident everyone would know it was God who gave the victory by simply seeing his uncut hair, much like someone who places a fish decal on the bumper of a Lexus. The driver may assume people will know by looking at the ornament that she believes God is responsible for her driving such a car. Those waiting at the bus stop as she drives by probably don't get the connection, but her weekly Bible study friends would. We need to be careful how we give God credit for what he does—or what we think he does—in our lives.

LEADERSHIP PRAYERS

Compare Samson's prayer with that of Deborah, the prophetess who judged Israel before Samson. She sang of God's victory over Sisera in great length. She prayed,

> So may all your enemies perish, O LORD!
> But may they who love you be like the sun
> When it rises in its strength.[69]

Or compare Judge Samson's prayer with King David's praises to God. The King prayed,

> I will sing a new song to you, O God;
> on the ten-stringed lyre I will make music to you,
> to the One who gives victory to kings,
> who delivers his servant David from the deadly sword.[70]

Give us aid against the enemy,
for the help of man is worthless.
With God we will gain the victory,
and he will trample down our enemies.[71]

David credited God with his victories and acknowledged God as his source of strength. He sometimes asked why God seemed to withdraw his hand in battle, but he always confessed his final trust in God as victor. He never claimed his efforts or strength as the reason for his success.

While Samson breathed a confession of God's help in his victory, his real prayer was, "Let's have some help down here—how about it?" He yelled, "Must I now die of thirst and fall into the hands of the uncircumcised?" Samson informed God that if he did not get a drink he would fall into enemy hands, and surely God would not want that. The foreshadowing in this statement warns the reader that Samson's lack of character, not God's lack of provision, would be the cause for him falling into the hands of his enemies. Samson prayed like a spoiled teenager reminding his father he was still the only son whom his father would never want to be harmed. "Thanks a lot for the help, Dad," says a son to the father who has just bailed him out of jail. "How about a little cash for the weekend?" God was Daddy's money to Samson. Little devotion and respect flowed from his mouth for the One who gave him life and victory.

I am not saying that you should refrain from asking God for what you need. King David asked for personal needs in his prayers. He cried out:

Contend, O LORD, with those who contend with me;
fight against those who fight against me.
Take up shield and buckler;
arise and come to my aid.[72]

He, however, also said prayers of submission to God that balanced prayers of need:

No king is saved by the size of his army;
no warrior escapes by his great strength.

A horse is a vain hope for deliverance;
despite all its great strength it cannot save.
But the eyes of the LORD are on those who fear him,
on those whose hope is in his unfailing love,
to deliver them from death
and keep them alive in famine.[73]

In Samson's prayer life, we see no signs of such balance. He prayed for his needs alone.

SAMSON'S ANSWERED PRAYER

God heard his hero's prayer: "Then God opened up the hollow place in Lehi, and water came out of it. When Samson drank, his strength returned and he revived." God answered his waning warrior's prayer. Reminiscent of God's response to Moses striking the rock out of selfish anger in the wilderness, here God caused water to flow from "the hollow place" near Samson. He drank. His strength returned. He was revived by God's gracious act.

The mystery to me is that if Samson's attitude in his prayer was so smug, why did God answer his request? Why didn't God scold him or correct him to address the Almighty with respect? Why not a "You don't talk to your father that way" speech followed by, "Ask nicely, and maybe I'll give it to you?" Why suddenly does there appear a spring in the desert if the spoiled child asked in such a manner?

The answer to those questions, I think, lies in the character of God, not that of his chosen one. Remember back to Samson's birth announcement? God told his parents through an angel that God had chosen him, "and he will begin the deliverance of Israel from the hands of the Philistines." God never reneges on his call, even when the chosen one chooses paths outside the design of God's purposes. For example, Samson chose to marry a non-Israelite woman. This was outside God's commandments for his people, and Samson's parents resisted the idea. However, God allowed it because his choice "was from the LORD, who was seeking an occasion to confront the Philistines, for at that time they were ruling over Israel."

God honors his call on our lives, not because of who we are but because of who he is and the eternal purposes he desires to accomplish through our lives. In this case, God may seem like a weak parent giving in to the whining of a spoiled child, but in reality, he is acting in accordance with his own character and accomplishing a plan to rescue all people, a plan that we can only see in part.

Samson's prayer revealed the heart of the supplicant as one selfish in his relationship with God. The answer to that prayer revealed the heart of God as the gracious provider for those he has chosen to fulfill his purposes, no matter their attitudes toward him. This statement challenges those who are convinced God only works with those who are righteous toward God before he responds to them. Some religious people may wonder how God could answer the prayers of someone so caught up in himself. Such sin surely negates the possibility of answered prayer. Yet God does not respond to us because of our piety. God responds to us out of his compassion and his plans to use us in his redemptive plans. Our righteousness does little to sway God in our direction. God has already given his heart to us in his Son.

How many times after a battle have I prayed like Samson? "Thank you for saving me through that crisis, but, Lord, I really could use . . . ." Those kinds of prayers remind me of the old Beatles tune, "I Me Mine." Or Alan Parson's "Let's Talk About Me." Too many of our prayers are more about our needs than about seeking God's plan and our part in it. The apostle Paul did not pray to get out of prison. He asked his friends to pray "that whenever I open my mouth, words may be given me so that I will fearlessly make known the mystery of the gospel, for which I am an ambassador in chains. Pray that I may declare it fearlessly, as I should."[74] Boldness *in* the circumstance, not deliverance from it, was his request.

Paul did pray that his "thorn in the flesh" be removed, but when God said "My grace is sufficient for you, for my power is made perfect in weakness," Paul humbly confessed, "Therefore I will boast all the more gladly about my weaknesses, so that Christ's power may rest on me. That is why, for Christ's sake, I delight in weaknesses, in insults, in hardships, in persecutions, in difficulties. For when I am weak, then I am strong."[75] A life submitted to the purposes of

God submits humbly to the circumstances of life because it is there that the follower of Jesus encounters the power of the Living Lord.

JESUS AT PRAYER

Jesus prayed, but his prayers were never about himself. You can argue his prayer in the Garden was about him, but while he did ask to be saved from crucifixion, he finally submitted to the purposes of God above his human desire to escape the pain of the Passion. Other than this intimate prayer with his Father before his death, Jesus prayed for others. He prayed for Jerusalem. He prayed for his disciples. He prayed in praise to his Father. Prayer was never about him or the pain he would endure.

Jesus' pattern of prayer seems to have been like moving between breathing normally and accelerated exercises of anaerobic huffing and puffing. He rhythmically engaged and withdrew from others to pray. Luke tells us that "Jesus often withdrew to lonely places and prayed"[76] It was after one of those nights of praying to the Father that his followers wanted him to teach them to pray. They discovered there was a correlation between the Teacher's all-night prayer vigils and the miracles he performed during the day.

Jesus taught them a simple prayer, and we recite it today like children who practice the scales in order someday to play Beethoven's Piano Concerto No. 4 in G Major, Op. 54. The Lord's Prayer is the model prayer because it leads our hearts to praise the Father, acknowledge his holiness, seek his will, and ask for our basic needs along with God's gracious forgiveness. Jesus' prayer tutors us to ask for Christ's spiritual guidance and rescue from the Evil One's schemes to ruin us. To pray Jesus' model prayer is to lead our thirsty hearts to drink at the spring of God's presence. There we are fed, embraced, and restored to return an engage the things of life with grace and humility.

Prayer was not an end-of-battle cry for more help from God with Jesus. It was a moment-by-moment conversation with the One who sent him. Prayer was a way of life that kept him prepared to engage those in need as well as those who would attack the Father's purposes for his life. While we often feel inclined to pray like Samson, we would do well to learn to pray like Jesus.

Sexual Urges

If Samson's prayers are a peek into his character, how he managed his sexual urges is a full-length documentary on his heart. Chapter 16 of Judges begins with Samson seeing a prostitute and going to her for the night. He found her in the Philistine-occupied city, Gaza, a coastal city that still plays a major role in world affairs today. Samson never tamed his desire for sex, so when he came to town, he looked to satisfy all of his appetites. I once read that the difference between appetite and hunger is that hunger is the physiological *need* for food and appetite is the psychological *perceived need* for food. Hunger keeps us alive. Appetite makes us obese.

Sex is a natural hunger God has placed in all of us. It becomes an appetite when there is no discipline to bridle it or satisfy it in God-designed ways. Samson, as we have seen, practiced little discipline in his life, so as he traveled through enemy territory, he saw a woman who sold her body with no strings attached, and he went to her to satisfy his appetite for sex.

The speaker in Proverbs warned young men:

Keep to a path far from her [the adulteress],
do not go near the door of her house,
lest you give your best strength to others
and your years to one who is cruel,
lest strangers feast on your wealth
and your toil enrich another man's house.
At the end of your life you will groan,
when your flesh and body are spent.
You will say, "How I hated discipline!
How my heart spurned correction!
I would not obey my teachers
or listen to my instructors.
I have come to the brink of utter ruin
in the midst of the whole assembly."[77]

These words clearly predict Samson's path as he continued his trips to foreign women. The cry of the last verses could have come from his mouth as he
died in the temple of Dagon: "I have come to the brink of utter ruin in the
midst of the whole assembly," a confession brought on by giving his strength
to a seductress.

Why was Samson always more interested in the women of Israel's enemies than in his own nation's women? His first wife, the prostitute of Gaza,
and Delilah, his final nemesis, were both Philistines. We never read of our
hero's interaction with women of his own country. Given that women were
treated as property in those days, maybe his lust for strange women came partially out of the desire to take other men's women. Affairs often start with a
man's desire to get what isn't his, what belongs to another man. It's possible
that Samson loved taking Philistine women as another way to show his superior strength over his enemies.

One key source of sexual roaming is pride. On the scorecard of an undisciplined male ego, the more women taken, the bigger the boast. And when a man
has difficulty finding women willing to compromise themselves for his brag-
ging rights, he has the option of turning to a prostitute. The Books of the Law
do not prohibit prostitution outright. The law did ban an Israelite becoming a
prostitute at a pagan shrine, and money earned by prostitution could not be
used to pay a vow.[78] Priests could not marry a woman who had practiced prostitution,[79] and by Jesus' day women who prostituted themselves were considered
religiously unclean. But, unlike Samson who used women, Jesus rescued prostitutes from the self-righteous scorn of religious leaders; Jesus showed gentleness
and compassion to these women. He also reestablished marriage as a sacred
institution in his day to curb the epidemic of divorce that arose because men
discarded their wives so freely.

Technically, Samson did not break any social law by going to a prostitute.
He was, however, violating the integrity of his calling. The angel told his parents, "No razor may be used on his head, because the boy is to be a Nazirite, set
apart to God from birth." The Hebrew term for Nazirite meant consecration,
devotion, and separation.

The signs of this separation with God included no cutting of the hair, no fermented drink, and no contact with the dead. Samson still had his hair, and we are not told of any alcoholic indulgence, but we know he had touched the carcass of a lion. Keeping two out of three religious rules makes you a good religious person.

Samson, it seems, didn't think going to prostitutes had anything to do with his devotion to God. His one try at conventional marriage hadn't gone so well, so maybe he thought this noncommittal release would be more practical. He may have rationalized like some do:

I keep most of the rules God gave me.

No one is perfect.

I'm successful in life, which is a sign of God's favor; and, after all, there are so many other restrictions on my life.

Carrying the weight of delivering God's people around all the time requires some release. Why not a little recreational sex to ease the burden of saving an entire nation?

We can always rationalize ways to wander away from God's purposes and plans.

Samson's sexual desires went undisciplined. Once again, he wanted what he saw. Chapter 14 of our tale began: "Samson went down to Timnah and saw there a young Philistine woman." He went home and told his mom and dad, "I have seen a Philistine woman in Timnah; now get her for me as my wife." Chapter 16 begins, "One day Samson went to Gaza, where he saw a prostitute. He went in to spend the night with her." He saw, desired, and got both women. Samson's actions fit perfectly in the era's zeitgeist when "every man did what was right in his own eyes."[80] With no acknowledgment of God's leadership and no clear authority to rule their hearts, people pursued what they saw fit to do by their own reasoning and rationale. Sounds like postmodern America to me.

John described this pattern of sin as "the cravings of sinful man, the lust of his eyes and the boasting of what he has and does [which] comes not from the Father but from the world."[81] Samson, according to John, was a man of the world. His cravings, lusts, and pride were part of his nature and drove him to cross the boundaries of God's plan for his life. He was unable to say no to the temptation of what he saw. His sinful "cravings," along with "the lust of his eyes" and his pride in his accomplishments, drove him into the house of a prostitute. Fredrick Buechner described lust as the craving of salt by a man dying of thirst.[82] Samson drank too much salt.

The prostitute did not ambush Samson. He was not some helpless youth caught unaware by a seductive mistress. Temptation seldom crashes over you like a tsunami. It more often seeps into your house like rising floodwaters from a hurricane's tidal surge. You know it's raining but do not check the drains. Soon you notice the basement is flooded, and you must get help or you're doomed to swim out by yourself. We let temptation into our lives either by laziness or design. God never does the tempting.[83] Giving in to temptation is our decisions to act on our desires.

Character—famously described as what we do when we think no one is watching—is built through discipline. Just as programs of exercise build muscle endurance, a daily regimen designed to curb the appetites and strengthen the spirit is the basis for success in spiritual matters. Dallas Willard reminds us that spiritual success doesn't come in a decision in the moment of the temptation but is summoned out of the daily practice of disciplines for the soul. The strength built up in daily exercises is how we overcome the temptation to step away from the flame of God's Presence onto the path of our own purposes.

Samson was strong and witty, but his appetites controlled him. He lacked character and the habits of life that build character. His parents never seem to have disciplined him. They gave him what he wanted when he asked, and as a young adult, their angel stepped out of the flame of God's purposes and took on life for himself. By the time he was an adult, he had no training to curb his appetites, so he became obese in desire.

What Do You Do with These Urges?

Jesus never married, nor did Jesus ever go to a prostitute to buy her services. He went to women trapped in selling their bodies to rescue them and to connect their hearts to their Father in heaven. Jesus honored women and served them in love. Where Samson used women, Jesus served them.

Jesus was not asexual. He was a man, "who has been tempted in every way, just as we are—yet was without sin."[84] Jesus experienced the normal sexual urges of a man, yet he did not cross any boundary the Father had drawn around his heart. Jesus channeled his sexual drives into his life on mission for God, which left little room for sexual relationships. He loved God above all, and his love for others flowed from that Source. Maybe a reason Jesus lived such a powerful life is because he rerouted the power of his sexuality and focused it like a laser on his mission to be a "ransom for many."[85] Jesus modeled for us what a life with every passion given to our Father in heaven can look like.

We live in a culture that presumes that the only outlet for our sexual urges is the physical act of sex in whatever form we want to express it. I believe that you can channel the power of sex into expressions other than through acts of sex. Music and art have close connections to our sexual drives. I have found the creative act of writing sometimes draws upon that part of me. Running and exercise can also tap into the power of that aspect of who I am, and those physical acts of exertion can calm the urges that my sexuality forces upon me. Contrary to popular opinion, when abstinence is appropriate or necessary, it is certainly possible. Redirecting sexual urges to creative acts can heighten those seasons of creativity with passion and insight. Celibacy is not punishment; it is a chosen discipline that directs God's gifts solely toward his calling for your life.

There are seasons of life when partners seem unequally matched in terms of sex drive. Perhaps one partner's needed medication reduces sexual desire, or one person is traveling for extended periods on business. What are people to do when their sex drives are flying on the interstate and their partners are parked in the garage? Let me be frank. If you find yourself in this situation, you can rationalize your need for sex and go find an outlet. That's how affairs start and how some of my friends have ruined their marriages. Another option is to meet your need with pornography, which is as available as Samson's prostitute in Gaza. Or you can stay committed to the one you love, redirect your urges, and cherish the moments you do share sexually. Please never tell me you need sex from another source because your spouse can't or won't deliver the goods any more. Marriage is more than sex. Love is more than a physical expression.

The difference between our two saviors is that Jesus devoted all of his urges to his mission, and he made spiritual exercises part of his everyday life. You see him freed from what the pangs of sexuality might have brought because he prayed, fasted, carved out times of solitude and silence, and studied the Scriptures. He served the poor and laughed with friends in authentic community. His power in public life came from his exercise of discipline in his private life. Jesus did not need the solace of a prostitute or sexual intimacy of a wife. The Father loved him, and in turn he loved the Father with all of his being.

Samson and Jesus give us two ways to handle our sexual urges. It is your option to choose which savior you want to emulate.

GATES OF THE CITY

God once again redeemed Samson's selfish choice for divine purposes. When the people of Gaza heard Samson was in town, they plotted to kill him. They planned to wait until the next morning to attack him as he left the prostitute's house. Samson, however, woke in the middle of the night and thought he'd exercise a little, so he tore the city gates from their pilings and carried them to the top of a hill—a hill thirty-eight miles away from Hebron! He would have fared well in the "World's Strongest Man" contests on cable television's ESPN2. Satisfied that he got what he wanted from the woman and that he had harassed the Philistines, he wandered back home.

The mercy of God is that although we make choices outside God's primary plans for our lives—even those of us who sense God's call on our lives—God redeems our actions for his purposes. The core hope in this tale is God's redeeming work in our lives. No matter the mistakes or blatant sins, God can turn our selfishness into acts of service for his purposes. This is a mystery to me. I want justice and fairness and a mechanical ethic that is predictable and efficient. But God gives me neither what I deserve nor what I desire on this. His withholding is grace, and before we ever meet Jesus on the pages of Scripture,

God continually demonstrated his grace toward those he chose—often, in spite of their sin and selfish ways.

Discussion Questions _____

1. Re-read the opening paragraph of this chapter. Do you agree or disagree with the author's observations? If you agree, how have you seen crisis and leisure reveal one's character?

2. When have you cried out to God in a crisis situation? How was your prayer like Samson's prayer? How was it more like David's prayer recorded in the chapter (pp. 88-90)?

3. How was God's answer to Samson's prayer evidence of the character of God?

4. Describe the difference between Samson's prayer and the prayers of Jesus?

5. How are sexual urges like hunger? What does the author suggest can be done to curb your sexual appetite? Which of these would you be willing to try?

6. How do you compare Jesus' sexuality with that of Samson?

Chapter Nine

DELILAH

*"Tell me the secret of your great strength and
how you can be tied up and subdued."*

—JUDGES 16:6

S ome time after the Gaza gate removal incident, Samson "fell in love with
a woman." Our hero fell in love. The big, strong man became weak in
the knees over a woman, a foreign woman named Delilah. Maybe our Hebrew
Hercules is a little bit like us after all. We can relate to the heart flutter that love
ignites. This is the first mention of love in Samson's life. We never hear of his
parent's love for him or even his love for his first wife—and significantly, we
never see testimony of love for God either. Love is not part of Samson's story
up to this point. Lust and want alone have been central to his relationships.

Yet what heroic saga would be complete without a woman who enraptures
the hero with love? Romeo had Juliet, Paris had Helen, and Samson had Delilah.
We are not told directly that Delilah was a Philistine, but she lived in the Valley
of Sorek, in a region ruled by the Philistines. She certainly was not a member
of any tribe of Israel. Samson's rogue behavior with foreign women continued
with his attraction for Delilah.

Given his past, I have to wonder if Samson's *love* was anything more than
infatuation, a giddy form of lust that convinces us our feelings are more than

daydreaming desire this time. Delilah's name meant "long hair hanging down" or "worshipper." Hey, maybe her long, hanging hair was the point of attraction for Samson. The couple's first conversation could have begun with a comment about the other's long hair, which could have led to talk about which comb best untangled their locks. "That's so strange. That's how I braid my hair," may have been part of the chitchat that made them think they were meant for each other. With nothing like God's designs to guide their desires, they were left to look for coincidences and emotions to judge the rightness of their newfound relationship.

I admit, I think Samson's love was passion on steroids. He had no benchmark for his feelings other than unbridled desire. For him, love was the adolescent hope of sex with a woman who said she wanted him, too. Love to our superhero was lust embraced by a woman with whom he wanted to stay with until morning. He thought he had found the woman of his fantasies. On the other hand, we never hear of Delilah's love for Samson. This was a one-way street of emotion. Lust does not require anything more than a willing accomplice. As long as Delilah allowed Samson into her bedroom, his love-like emotions soared.

Then again, Delilah may have suffered from her own form of infatuation. Being loved by your country's Most Wanted brings notoriety. Bonnie may have held on to Clyde because of whom he made her, rather than how she cared for him. Some of Hollywood's couples are more about appearance and notoriety than love. People suspect Michael Jackson and Lisa Marie Presley married more out of need for what the other could do for their careers than about love and romance, and the public has speculated similarly about plenty of other couples. We find out soon from our storyteller that Delilah's feelings for Samson were only skin deep. Money and power weighed more in her value system than her love for Samson. This relationship may not have been a publicity stunt but it definitely became about the money.

Samson's relationship was empty of the sacrifice, care, and patience true love carries. Just as his path as a savior was void of godly character, his relationships were absent of genuine love.

JESUS AND WOMEN

Jesus never made women the objects of his physical desires, but he always showed them love. While Samson modeled a man's craving to attract and conquer women, Jesus showed us how to serve them. He defended the woman who poured perfume on his feet against the religious prejudice of his host. He stood between the woman caught in adultery and self-righteous religious leaders. He reminded those who held stones in their hands that no one was without sin, and if any of them could honestly say otherwise, they could have the opening-game pitch—a challenge that, of course, no one could take. Jesus talked to the woman of seven husbands at the town well in the middle of the day. That conversation broke every social, racial, and religious rule of his day. He healed her seeking heart, and she became a troubadour of God's love in her hometown. He healed a mother's son in Nain and bantered with a foreign woman who begged for his blessing. Jesus never turned a woman away who sought him, and Dr. Luke tells us many women followed and supported our Savior.

This was the difference between Jesus' love for women and Samson's desire for them. Jesus' love for women grew out of the Father's love in his Son's heart. Jesus came to serve not to be served. Samson was sent for the same reason, but he missed the message.

Jesus demonstrated the Love that sent him to men and women alike. Love embodied by Christ is service to the heart needs of others regardless of their status, beauty, or ability to reciprocate. Love is not seducing someone to get whom you want next to you in bed. Love is laying down your life for others. To me, marriage is a man laying down his life for the woman who lays down her life for him. Mutual sacrifices, unrequited service, and friendship built upon shared pain and ecstasy are the colors of a marriage painted in Christ's love.

SEX AND MARRIAGE

One dimension of sex is the act of service, meeting the physical needs of your spouse. Thinking of sex as a giving act keeps each encounter from becoming self-centered. Healthy sex in marriage is other-centered, giving and not taking from one's spouse. The partner being served, not the stronger or more imaginative of the two, draws the boundaries. This model of sex flies in the face of porn peddlers and filmmakers who sell sex as a remedy to satisfy a person's sexual desires.

Paul, the Pharisee-turned-Christ follower, knew the importance of partners satisfying each other in order to serve with each other. His insight leads some to speculate that he may have lost his wife to death or in his decision to follow Jesus into the mission field. Like other mission-driven apostles who would follow in his steps, during the time we know him, he preferred to serve Jesus without the obligations of marriage. He was wise enough, however, to know this state of affairs was not for everyone. He advised the hedonistic Corinthians:

> The husband should fulfill his marital duty to his wife, and likewise the wife to her husband. The wife's body does not belong to her alone but also to her husband. In the same way, the husband's body does not belong to him alone but also to his wife. Do not deprive each other except by mutual consent and for a time, so that you may devote yourselves to prayer. Then come together again so that Satan will not tempt you because of your lack of self-control.[86]

God's plan for physical fulfillment is that sex serves both spouses' needs, freeing a husband and wife to work together spiritually. Mutual consent to set aside sex in order to practice the spiritual discipline of prayer is on few marriage agendas today, but a couple truly shares a life-calling and not just a bed when they make these kinds of decisions.

Samson demonstrated the opposite of this ideal. Sex was all about his needs when he had them or when he wanted to feed them. Putting sex on hold in order to do anything else didn't seem to fall on his radar.

TREACHEROUS LOVE

Funny how personal history repeats itself. Like an alcoholic who unconsciously creates the same scenarios of self-destruction over and over again, Samson fell in love with a woman whose loyalty was greater to her kinsmen than to him. His tryst with Delilah was a game of poker with a bigger pot. His first wife cost him thirty dead men's clothes. His match with this lover would cost him his life.

Samson's relationship with Delilah attracted the attention of the rich and powerful. We are told that "the rulers of the Philistines went to her." These weren't brothers or cousins or even local officials. These were the political leaders of the regional cities, and they would pay huge sums of money to find out what made Samson so strong. Every man has a weakness, and they would pay dearly to discover Samson's source of strength so they could remove this menace from the scene. They each offered Delilah "eleven hundred pieces of silver" if she would "lure [Samson] into showing [her] the secret of his great strength and how [they could] overpower him so [they] may tie him up and subdue him." Delilah does not seem to be tortured with any sort of moral dilemma or personal angst when offered the money. She didn't say, "Give me a day, and I'll get back to you," or offer a simple, "Let me think about it." She didn't even negotiate for more. Next thing we read is that she asked Samson for his secret.

Was Delilah wicked or did she just see this as a way to improve her place in life? I don't see Delilah as any more evil than people today who let money seduce them into selling their moral core to get more stuff they'll leave behind when they die. With no hope of heaven, we are left to pillage for all we can get here. Paul agreed that the Epicureans were right if there was no resurrection. "Let us eat and drink, for tomorrow we die"[87] was their fraternity motto. Delilah was a willing accomplice in the economy of power. She wasn't any more corrupt than some in the halls of power today. She simply possessed savvy for survival. This is the only way to live when God claims no leadership in your life.

Delilah could not get past eleven hundred pieces of silver from each of the rulers. Just as she was about to become Samson's temptress, money and power were her tempters. Maybe these had become a way of life for Delilah: her beauty enticed men to get what she wanted, and she allowed herself to be used as long as she could use others for what she wanted. The rulers used her. She used Samson. Samson gives up the secret of his strength to satisfy the love of his life, and everyone goes home happy.

And after all the transactions, the rulers will stay trapped in their quest to retain power, Delilah will remain chained to her beauty-for-hire lifestyle, and Samson will stumble blindly to his death. Solomon was right when he wrote, "When a wicked man dies, his hope perishes; all he expected from his power comes to nothing."[88]

STALKING THE PREY

Delilah immediately began to stalk her prey. I see her smiling flirtatiously, tracing a lock of hair down her suitor's cheek, winking, and singing seductively, "Tell me the secret of your great strength and how you can be tied up and subdued." She could have passed as courtesan Satine in the film *Moulin Rouge*, who sold her body to finance her dreams.

Samson loved to toy with the secret of his strength. His hair made him powerful, yet it came to possess him and ultimately to destroy him. With it, he had never lost a battle or skirmish, and he had inflicted huge losses on his enemies. He had been told he would win because he was chosen by God to be Israel's deliverer. His bravado suggests that he believed nothing could stop him. Why not play with the deepest secret of his life? He couldn't lose. So he thought.

Samson reduced the source of his strength to the length of his hair, not to God who truly gave it to him. He had violated every other guideline God had given his parents but this one. All that remained of his Nazirite vows was his long hair. When we reduce God's power to a single aspect of our calling, we are in danger of being seduced by a Delilah who can quench the flame of our life's purpose.

For example, I believe God's mission call on my life is to lead others on the mission to help people trust Jesus. Preaching is part of that call. It is the most visible part of what I do, and it is where I receive the most compliments—and criticisms. If I were to reduce God's call on my life to preaching and make that my best effort and bask in what others tell me, I would set myself up for a fall. The opinions of the day would determine my feelings of whether or not I was fulfilling my call. But my calling is more than preaching, and the power of my ministry rests in my relationships with people in the daily sharing of life together, not in my weekend presentations. To neglect the power of relationships for the perceived power of my preaching is to announce to God I have chosen how he best can use me. Samson reduced his call to the length of his hair, and in doing so, he narrowed the ways in which God could protect and empower him.

Samson deceitfully whispered to his lover, "If anyone ties me with seven fresh thongs that have not been dried, I'll become as weak as any other man." He seems to have thought if he gave her something, then he could get what he wanted. The bartering to get what each one wanted had begun, like shoppers at an open-air market. All he wanted was to sleep with her. All she wanted was the money. Any advice columnist could see where this relationship was headed.

The detail of Samson's lie is admirable. Lying was part of his love for riddles. Details make lies believable, and Samson did a good job of giving the details of this story. He said that to tie him up with seven thongs that had not been dried was the secret of his strength. The word "thongs" here means bowstrings, which were made of ox gut and required time to dry before they were stretched across a bow. He had to chuckle in the back of his mind to think of men tying him up with animal intestines.

"Why not," Delilah may have mused when she heard his answer. "Who knows but whether some unknown god has put magic in ox entrails?"

A Servant Leader

Why did Samson start his flight toward disaster so easily? One reason is that he still had no understanding of the larger script in which he was an actor. John Eldredge reminds us we have fallen into a greater epic, one that has been going on long before we came on the scene. He tells us the secret to life is to discover we have a crucial role to play in the Story and then to live out that role. He writes, "We won't begin to understand our lives, or what this so-called gospel is that Christianity speaks of, until we understand the Story in which we have found ourselves."[89] That Story is God's efforts to rescue us from the Evil One and to set us into the rightful roles he has us play in the eternal saga for the hearts of all people. The Epic is the story of our lives.

Samson seemed to have no sense of his part in God's Story. He never acted like he had a part to play in the covenant God had made with Israel. He felt no connection with the judges who had served before him. His battles were his own, and his passions were self-directed. Serving others in the name of the Lord who called him was never a core value in his life; Samson would rather work alone.

Samson failed to be a servant leader like Jesus because he never made himself a servant to God's mission call on his life. His parents surely told him of an angel in the flame that announced his birth and the unique part he would play in Israel's story with God. He clearly had become more intrigued with the mystique than with the calling the messenger brought from heaven. His parents must have told him the bigger story of God's covenant with his people, yet Samson seemed to have no context for his strength and wit. He could not see his place in the line of servant leaders whom God had chosen to move his redemptive purposes closer to the cross of Jesus.

Servant leadership begins with a clear mission. Samson's mission was to "begin the deliverance of Israel from the hands of the Philistines." Yes, he became a fly in the ointment of Israel's enemy, but he never made himself servant to that mission. His life was not about completing the mission. It was all about using his strength for his own desires. Therefore, Samson never became a leader who led by serving others to complete that mission. He was a hero but not a servant leader. He neither served nor equipped others to complete the God-given mission for their lives.

Samson never learned his place in God's history because he never caught that truth from his family as he matured. His family worshipped God like so many in America today. God was part of Israel's culture. Worshipping God, tithing crops and herds, and observing the festivals were built into the rhythms of daily life. Their communities were plotted by tribal boundaries, and their faith had been handed down to them in traditions that had lost their meaning. The cost of the covenant had long left their memories. The wilderness wanderings were stories told by old men at the city gate. Many lived out a hollow faith that had been sewn into their culture like a single thread into a multi-colored garment. Few could follow it through the pattern of everyday life. Israel went through the motions and all Samson caught were those motions.

The message from Mom and Dad that he was set apart for God's greater purposes seemed only to register as religious habits he laid aside when he became an adult. The concept of covenant—God's undying love toward those he had chosen—lay neglected. Nothing of its depth and meaning permeated Samson's psyche. Without mission, there is no leadership. Without a servant's heart, there can be no service to the greater good.

Jesus knew his mission. If his parents told him of the angel's visit, they seem also to have told him of his purpose for being on the earth. I imagine Joseph told his son how he got his name, and then of Joshua, his namesake, and the other leaders God chose to establish Israel as God's people, and then of his other name, Emanuel, God with us. Jesus clearly got the message. Faith was more than a habit for Jesus' family, and he caught the deeper meaning that was connected with trips to Jerusalem and daily rituals of faith. Unlike Samson, Jesus knew his role in God's script for the rescue of the human race.

Jesus gave his life for God's mission call. Nothing Jesus did was about his life on earth. Every move he made had eternal consequences for all people. He declared in his home synagogue,

> The Spirit of the Lord is on me,
>   because he has anointed me
>   to preach good news to the poor.
>
> He has sent me to proclaim freedom for the prisoners
>   and recovery of sight for the blind,
>   to release the oppressed,
>   to proclaim the year of the Lord's favor.[90]

Later in his ministry he announced he had come "to seek and to save those who were lost."[91] Jesus knew his mission and lived to complete it. Samson had a mission, but he never got around to giving himself to it wholly.

One of the clearest statements Jesus made about his reason for being was after a leadership lesson to his twelve apprentices. He had told them, "Whoever wants to become great among you must be your servant, and whoever wants to be first must be slave of all." His followers understood "great" and "first," but they struggled to connect "servant" and "slave" to greatness. Jesus went on to quietly state his mission, "For even the Son of Man did not come to be served, but to serve, and to give his life as a ransom for many."[92] Jesus knew what his life and death counted for. He set aside all personal desires and ambition to fulfill his purpose in coming to earth. He became our Savior because he kept his eye on the Father's mission.

Those who know their mission and give themselves to it are those who make history. Its currents carry the rest of humanity along.

ANOTHER TRY

Delilah believed her new lover. She passed the word on to her benefactors, and they got her what she wanted—not because they cared for her, but because they wanted their enemy. Remember, everyone in this story is playing for his or her own benefit. Delilah arranged for the rulers' thugs to hide in the room while she seductively tied Samson in the seven fresh bowstrings they supplied.

"Samson, the Philistines are upon you!" Delilah then cried out.

He braced to defend himself, and "he snapped the thongs as easily as a piece of string snaps when it comes close to a flame." We can imagine the goons in the room jumping back from the freed strong man and running for the door, sprinting to their bosses and telling of the failed capture attempt. The higher-ups were not worried. They knew Delilah would get the job done.

Our storyteller observed, "so the secret of his strength was not discovered." I don't believe our chronicler wrote this line with a sigh of relief. It sounds to me more like a warning to the reader that Samson had only dodged another bullet. Our hero's enemy was not out of ammo, and he was too self-centered to be trusted. His ego had trumped the right choice too often before. Picture the scene like a game of Texas Hold 'Em, with Samson saying, "Lost that hand. I didn't read the cards right that time. No problem. I still have chips. I'm in." And Delilah anted up and waited for her next cards to be dealt.

The writer's choice of simile is odd here. He tells us the bowstrings broke as easily as string near a flame. Is our storyteller reminding us of the flame that consumed the angel at Samson's birth announcement? Or is he foreshadowing Samson's demise like a moth that flies too close to a candle's flame? Is he telling us Samson is more like a string near the flame than an angel in the flame? Is he warning each of us that our place is as God's messenger in the fire of God's purpose, and if we step out of that place, our lives become like that string? The irony is that the flame of empowerment can too often turn into the flame of judgment.

After Samson defeated the bowstrings, Delilah protested. I can imagine her pushing out her lower lip and looking up at Samson with her big brown eyes as she said, "You have made a fool of me; you lied to me. Come now, tell me how you can be tied."

And Samson, it seems, did not hesitate. He could see the game. A riddle. A woman. Gangsters hidden in the room for an ambush. He had won this game before. Adrenaline raced through his veins. He blurted out another idea—one that had worked in his favor before: "If anyone ties me securely with new ropes that have never been used, I'll become as weak as any other man."

Of course, when Samson's countrymen had tied him in new ropes to deliver him to the Philistines, he had broken free to kill a thousand of Israel's enemies. I suppose the memory of his greatest achievement delighted him. But trying to repeat past victories leads only to future disasters. Life never offers the same rosters and stadium a second time. You can never orchestrate a win like the 2004 Boston Red Sox over the New York Yankees in Game Seven of the ALCS or the Manning brothers winning back-to-back Superbowls and carrying home MVP trophies. Samson thought he could pull off the same miracle twice.

Weaving a Web

Delilah took the bait and tied him up. She wrapped up Samson with the new rope like a female black widow spider might spin her silk around her partner after mating only to eat him later. For the mating female, once the male spider has served his purpose and she can lay eggs and mother her brood, she no longer needs the male, so she often eats him to nourish her offspring. Delilah treated her Israelite mate the same way. When he was wrapped in her web, she would have her wealth and status among the powerful. Samson would have served his purpose, and he would become someone's dinner.

Delilah called out the same warning as before, "Samson, the Philistines are upon you!" Samson responded as before: "He snapped the ropes off his arms as if they were threads." Rope became like thread and bowstring like singed string compared to Samson's physical strength. His strength of character, however, lacked the same potency.

Delilah seems fed up with playing the conniving partner. Here I imagine her cheeks flushed with frustration, her heart beating with a passion to seize her day. She would not be denied this chance to secure her future. She now cornered her prey saying, "Until now, you have been making a fool of me and lying to me. Tell me how you can be tied." Yes, Samson had made a fool of her.

One might think Samson was running out of ideas. But then, he was known for his wit and imagination. He couldn't lose this hand. His opponent was relentless. He concocted an extravagant plan, one to match her persistence. This idea was so outlandish she would have to cling to him to know the truth. He also must have thought she would tire of the game. Truth was never Samson's first option. It couldn't be. He was seldom in a place where it mattered. So Samson gave Delilah a task that would occupy her for some time, which seemed to matter in the game of survival.

"If you weave the seven braids of my head into the fabric on the loom and tighten it with the pin, I'll become as weak as any other man." Delilah went right to work. As soon as he fell asleep, Spider Woman wove his hair into a piece of fabric. Maybe he dreamed of their embrace as he lay in her lap, while she daydreamed of what she would do with the bounty money. Hearts that hide their true dreams never become one.

When she had finished the first "hair 'n thread" weave pattern, Delilah shouted again that the Philistines were upon the Israelite. For a third time, he broke the bonds she placed upon him. For a third time, the thugs ran. Samson seems to have thrived on the game they played. Delilah, though, was growing tired of it all, and she became angry. She had no idea (or did she?) that anger was what broke Samson when his first wife wanted to know the secret of his wedding riddle, but Delilah played the part well.

Breaking Down

Delilah stomped her feet and cried, "How can you say, 'I love you,' when you won't confide in me? This is the third time you have made a fool of me and haven't told me the secret of your great strength." By dropping the "How can you say, 'I love you'?" bomb, Delilah articulated that love in this relationship meant "you love me when you give me what I want." Given that definition of love, Samson couldn't say he loved her if he didn't give her what she asked. True love, of course, does not operate in the arena of "you scratch my back, I'll scratch yours." Love does not play those games. It is dead serious. Lives are at stake. To play with the heart of another is not an option for those who truly love.

Remember what drove Samson to give into his now burned-to-death first wife? "She cried the whole seven days of the feast. So on the seventh day he finally told her, because she continued to press him." Her persistent crying broke him down. Delilah either had a strong intuition about Samson's weakness to whining or she had heard stories that tailed the Israelite hero to her bed. Either way, "With such nagging she prodded him day after day until he was tired to death." The Message summarizes Samson's response this way: "Finally, he was fed up—he couldn't take another minute of it." For a second time in this savior's relationships, his partner's nagging and whining led to giving up his secret. This time, however, he gave up the secret to the strength of his calling. And when the text says he was "tired to death," we know the words are ominously accurate. What he told Delilah would *be* his death.

"So he told her everything," our storyteller relates. Like Esau who gave up his inheritance for a bowl of soup, Samson gave up his calling for peace and quiet. Esau's stomach and Samson's desire for quiet drove them to give up that which God had given them: parts that were uniquely theirs in the Story of God. One gave up his birthright. The other squandered the strength of his calling. Neither made a trade of equal value.

How can you give up your birthright for a bowl of soup? How can you trade the secret of your strength for peace and quiet? Ask anyone who has traded his marriage for an affair or success for his family. Our ancient hero's choices don't seem that odd when compared to the options many people choose every day, bartering family for promotions, selling out marriages for infatuations. We are all tempted, at some point or another, to give up God's eternal purposes to satisfy temporary human urges. We must be careful when we criticize Samson's choice if we have not installed firewalls around our hearts.

Samson blurted out the outward source of strength in his life, "No razor has ever been used on my head," he said, "because I have been a Nazirite set apart to God since birth. If my head were shaved, my strength would leave me, and I would become as weak as any other man." The confession of his calling rolled off his tongue so freely. *I have been a Nazirite set apart to God since birth.* Samson knew his calling, the flame that enveloped his life, yet it had become as empty in meaning as some confess today, "I'm a Christian." The sentence is simple and people can say it a million times, but it means nothing more than an empty phrase. The words are partially true, but the life that was to carry them out is void of their power and purpose.

When asked only once by the religious leaders, "Are you the Christ?" and once by Pilate, "Are you the king of the Jews?" Jesus answered, "Yes, it is as you say."[93] He didn't have to make the confessions for them. He simply answered what they accused him of being. Jesus' life led others to confess his identity for him. Samson's life was so foreign to his confession he had to tell it as though it were a secret. Jesus's life and teachings backed up the purpose for which he had come, and he lived to bring glory to God. Only in private in order to silence a desperate woman did Samson speak the truth of his strength. We too often confess our allegiance to Jesus like Samson confessed his identity—we tell our secret when we believe it will work for our advantage, not as the foundation upon which we build our lives.

Jesus called his apprentices to follow his example. Their lives were their confession of allegiance to him. The flame of God's presence surrounding them would be a light to others that they could not hide. Jesus told them,

> You are the light of the world. A city on a hill cannot be hidden. Neither do people light a lamp and put it under a bowl. Instead they put it on its stand, and it gives light to everyone in the house. In the same way, let your light shine before men, that they may see your good deeds and praise your Father in heaven.[94]

Paul, when challenged by his opponents to produce letters of recommendation to support his claims of apostleship, wrote

> Are we beginning to commend ourselves again? Or do we need, like some people, letters of recommendation to you or from you? You yourselves are our letter, written on our hearts, known and read by everybody. You show that you are a letter from Christ, the result of our ministry, written not with ink but with the Spirit of the living God, not on tablets of stone but on tablets of human hearts.[95]

People, not accolades on parchment, were proof of Paul's spiritual work in Corinth. He did not need a letter with a seal of approval to show how God used him. Changed lives were all he needed to point to as evidence he did what God had called him to do.

How much freer would you and I be if we would depend on our investments in people's lives to be our letters of recommendation? If we are always seeking recognition that we can carry as proofs in our pockets, we will never be satisfied. That will only lead to an endless pursuit of getting ahead. All God wants from us is to be messengers in the flame of his love who serve others. I don't have to point to the size of my church's campus or its budget to gain recommendations as one who is fulfilling God's call on my life. I point to people who no longer are addicted to alcohol or a career, people who have given up ownership of all they have and joyfully give to the needs of others, people who once were lost but now are found. These are the proof of my calling to which I hold.

TRAITORS

Samson's secret had slipped out. It was as if he was in the heat of an argument in the conference room and blurted out what he really thought about the boss—to the boss! At such a moment, everyone stops talking. All you can hear is the hum of the copier in the workroom. His peers know he has said what he thought about the boss all along; he's made his feelings clear around the water cooler. He tries to cover what he said with another topic, but everyone sees his flushed face and darting eyes. They know he's trapped by his own words. He's busted. Empty the desk. Today is his last day at the office.

Samson stood still. Delilah knew this was the truth. The Bible says, "When Delilah saw that he had told her everything, she sent word to the rulers of the Philistines, 'Come back once more; he has told me everything.'" She saw it in his face. She had not known the strong man long, but she read in his eyes that he was not lying this time. I imagine she kissed him on the cheek like Judas kissed Jesus on the night he betrayed his Savior and sent a messenger to those who financed the bust. The Philistine rulers must have believed this was the real deal, because they returned "with the silver in their hands."

Both saviors had betrayers. Samson had Delilah. Jesus had Judas. Delilah was a friend of Samson's enemies, and she wanted to gain wealth and power by bringing down the menace to her people. We can accept her seduction and betrayal as an act of patriotism. Samson was the stupid one. Delilah was just getting by. Samson was supposed to be the one on mission.

Judas is another story. He was on the same side as Jesus. He was in Jesus' inner circle of leadership. Like George Washington's friend Benedict Arnold who betrayed his country and ended up a ranking officer in the enemy's army, Judas's betrayal was especially hideous because he gave his friend over to their mutual enemies. We have a hard time finding a good reason for Judas's kiss of betrayal. I have heard some suspect that Judas wanted to force Jesus' hand so he would confront the Romans and set up his earthly kingdom. If this was his motivation, his blunder was that he made his deal with the religious leaders, and they had no intention of using Jesus to free Israel from the Romans. They liked things just the way they were. Judas tried to bring in the kingdom of God by betraying its king. The religious leaders wanted this so-called savior out of their hair so they could get on with their lives of power and influence.

The irony of Delilah's and Judas's betrayals is that God used both of them to accomplish his ultimate will. God used Delilah's treachery to hand Samson over to the Philistines to help in the deliverance of Israel. God used Judas's conniving to hand Jesus over to finish the deliverance of all people. Those who serve their own purposes cannot reroute the purposes of God. Sometimes those selfish pursuits become the conduit through which God's purposes flow. This is a mystery too great to understand.

A Sheared Savior

Delilah put Samson to sleep on her lap by playing with the hair of his strength. She may have sung a lullaby as she stroked his hair. Rather than leaving in shame for telling his secret, Samson may have slept soundly in relief. What he had worked so hard to hide was now exposed. He was weary of carrying the weight around for so long, and sleep was easier than confronting the consequences of his sin.

Seeking the path of least resistance instead of the hard work of truthtelling had become a pattern from which Samson could no longer escape. His disobedience was complete. He had violated every requirement to be a Nazirite. So why not sleep? I pray he was not so simple as to think Delilah would not do anything with the information he gave her. Three other times she had come back to the table after he had won the hand. Why wouldn't she do the same now?

Samson may have reasoned that even though she cut his hair, he would be able to survive the onslaught of his enemies. How could he think that way? Once again, the answer is pride. Samson placed his faith not in God's power but in his own abilities. His ego had finally convinced him that even if he violated

God's calling on his life, he could still be a superhero. He had stayed strong after breaking the other rules. Hubris heightened his confidence in his own strength. But God's Word does not change with our attitudes toward it.

Samson slept while Delilah toyed with his hair and an unknown accomplice shaved off his seven braids. He slept like a baby in his bed of pride while a nameless barber removed the hair that had not been cut since birth. "And his strength left him" is all our storyteller needed to write. We know in our heads that to violate God's rules leads to our destruction. We scowl at Samson's haughty attitude, but we too compromise our call by thinking, like him, that we will be okay if we live dually in our pride and in the ways of God.

"He awoke from his sleep and thought, 'I'll go out as before and shake myself free.' But he did not know that the LORD had left him." Samson awoke a sheared sheep, a sheep about to be led to slaughter, but he was clueless that "the LORD had left him." How does someone miss that? Had he become so insensitive to the things of God that he could not tell the flame had flickered and gone out? Had his soul become callous to the power of God because sin had replaced service to God in his heart? How do you miss something as significant as the Lord leaving you?

Then again, if we reflect, maybe we'll find that it's not so hard after all. I know I go through times when my faith and ministry become routine. Church members are content. We are paying the bills. New members are joining, and there are no weeds in the church lawn. During those days, my mind wanders to other interests. I watch television more than I pray. I spend more time with friends than with those who need the love of Christ. All the while, I am getting spiritually flabby, and the Spirit has no room to work. Over a lifetime of such routine, I believe I could come to a place to where I "did not know that the LORD had left" me. I would stand to proclaim the Word or pray against the powers of evil and my words would fall flat and my prayers would bounce off the invading spirits like rubber arrows in a cartoon. Yes, the flame of God's calling can go out unaware.

Jesus never lost contact with the Father. His flame never flickered but always burned strongly because Jesus never ventured into the arena of living for himself while trying to look like he lived for his Father. Jesus spent nights in prayer. He made room in his life for the Father to speak—and room for himself to listen. Jesus was so sensitive to the power of the Father in his life that when a woman whose body would not stop bleeding touched his garment "at once Jesus realized that power had gone out from him."[96] Jesus turned and asked who had touched him. When the woman came forward, Jesus didn't scold her; he healed her. Samson lacked that kind of spiritual sensitivity.

Delilah coaxed Samson's secret from him, and he was so spiritually numb he didn't even realize what had happened. Now all that was left for her to collect her newfound wealth was to hand him over to his enemies.

Discussion Questions

1. How would you describe the difference between infatuation and love?

2. Compare Jesus' love toward women and Samson's behavior toward the women he loved?

3. How does the author describe sex in marriage as an act of service to one's spouse? Explain your feelings or thoughts about this concept.

4. According to the author, how was Samson more a hero than a servant leader? How was Jesus our model of servant leadership?

5. Compare Jesus' confession of who he was with Samson telling the secret of his strength to Delilah. How does the author distinguish between the two?

6.   Have you ever felt the Lord has left you? What were the circumstances
     and how did you return to an assurance of his presence?

Chapter Ten

HERO OR SAVIOR?

"O Sovereign LORD, remember me.
O God, please strengthen me just once more,
and let me with one blow get revenge
on the Philistines for my two eyes. "

— JUDGES 16:28

S ocrates drank hemlock after he could no longer reason his way out of justice by his peers. Tradition has it St. Peter was crucified upside down in Rome because he felt he was not worthy to die like his Master. Napoleon wasted away on the island of St. Helena after his defeat at Waterloo. Hitler committed suicide with his newly wed mistress in Berlin as the Soviet army entered the city. In 1997, thirty-eight devotees along with their leader Marshall Herff Applewhite drank to their deaths hoping to enter an alien spaceship following the Hale-Bopp comet. Samson died under a pile of pagan temple stones. Jesus died hoisted on a Roman death machine.

Death is more than simply an epitaph to one's life. It is more than a marker for historians to record a person's time on the planet. How one dies is part of why one lives, and it often reveals the true mission and meaning of a person's life. Some deaths are dramatically tragic and ill-timed. Other deaths are clearly purposeful, as portrayed in John Irving's *A Prayer for Owen Meany*. And some deaths provide lessons for the rest of us, as with Mitch Albom's *Tuesdays with Morrie*.

Samson's life ended more like a tragic ending to an epic tale than a purposeful end to a purpose-driven life. Unlike Irving's Owen Meany, who knew he was an "instrument of God," Samson never seemed to grasp the significance of his life nor the power of his life. This savior's story ended after everyone cleaned up the mess he made and went home. After Samson's death, our storyteller simply begins a new paragraph with a new character, and we read on. There is nothing to memorialize in his dying. His flame flickered out. Another one was lit. The story continues.

Samson chose his end. He seized an opportunity to avenge his pride. Some would call his death heroic, like a prisoner of war taking the gun of a guard and killing several enemy captors before he is gunned down. But when we perform an autopsy on our hero's heart, we see that his actions were selfish, not motivated by loyalty to his mission and comrades. Samson's death was consistent with how he lived. No surprises or last minute twists in this tale's plot. We've seen his misspent death coming for some time.

CAPTURED

After Delilah's final betrayal, Samson's enemies "seized him, gouged out his eyes and took him down to Gaza." The Philistines led their shaved, blinded, and humiliated captive to the city where he had torn off its gates and carried them into the hills. The townspeople may have wondered what had happened to the man who had once left with their city gates on his back in the middle of the night. Can't you imagine that when he was led through the city streets bound and blind, the people whispered to one another, "What happened to his strength?" or shouted to his captors, "How'd you capture him?"

The people of Jerusalem must have wondered the same things as Jesus was led to the cross. Days earlier, crowds praised him as the Messiah with palm branches and hosannas. He was the promised king riding on a gentle donkey just as it had been prophesied centuries before. A week later, as he stumbled subdued and barely able to take his next step, many in the crowds must have reeled in confusion and pain with him. To them, he was their next chance for Israel to be freed from the Romans and now he carried his own execution tree on his back. Both Jerusalem and Gaza wondered what had happened to the men who days before were larger than life, stronger than all, kings of their destinies.

While the crowds mused about how the strong man was captured, we know Samson was on a death march because of his self-worshipping pride. He got himself into this mess. A cloud of justice hovered over the military unit that delivered Samson to the authorities. He was captured, and he was about to get what his enemies thought he deserved. No Geneva Convention standards were there to protect him; suffering beating, humiliation, and the loss of his eyes was part of his losing the battle. Samson's epic feats and spectacular strength didn't matter to the people or their leaders—everyone knew the Israelite enemy was about to get his due. The Philistines had triumphed once more over Israel.

Jesus, on the other hand, was not a captured enemy of the state. That charge was one piece of the mockery of his execution. The man who healed the sick, cast out demons, and never spoke of rebellion against Rome was on the path to his death not because of the Roman government, but because the religious leaders of his own community orchestrated his execution. Like so many other religious groups who have destroyed the saviors of their times to maintain the status quo, the religious leaders in Jesus' community meticulously calculated his removal.

Jesus still threatens institutional religion today. His ways and teachings don't fit into organized anything, and when we try to squeeze them into programs and calendars they mess up cash flow and stability, two things that are essential to an organization. Jesus was no threat to Rome, an empire that had put down many rebellions along the way to world domination. Jesus was not leading a militant insurgent group; he posed no threat of violence to Rome.

No, it was Jesus' attack on his own people's religious leaders and their attitude of possessing God that put him on the trail to crucifixion. These leaders had been chosen to be conduits of God's purposes to the world, and they held that privilege as their exclusive right. They beat and killed Jesus because he introduced an entirely new way of relating to God into a toxic system of religion.

The crowd at Jesus' death march was confused at how such a thing could have happened. The secret was he had allowed it all to happen. Jesus told his disciples, "I am the good shepherd. The good shepherd lays down his life for the sheep. . . . No one takes it from me, but I lay it down of my own accord. I have authority to lay it down and authority to take it up again."[97] Jesus' death was part of the Plan begun before Creation. The One whose birth was announced by angels and whose life sparked the flames of God's presence, was on his way to complete his mission as he climbed the hill called the Skull.

Samson had been trapped by his pride. He took his life only after he had toyed with those who had imprisoned him. It seems fair to assume that he would rather have been in bed with Delilah. Jesus lay down his life and allowed his capture. The cross was his bed, and he humbly submitted to the mission he had been sent to finish. Samson was sucked into the vortex of his own desires, and his life ended short of what God had planned for him.

Humiliation

"Binding him with bronze shackles," the Philistines "set [Samson] to grinding in the prison." Once free to roam where his passions led him, his enemies shackled Samson and forced him to do the work of women. No longer did he dominate women. He now did their work of grinding grain into flour. When I was growing up, I saw pictures of Samson pushing an apparatus alongside an ox that crushed grain. He still looked like a strong man doing the work of animals. I was impressed he was so strong even though he was blind and chained. But a more authentic picture is that he sat on the floor grinding wheat kernels between rocks.[98] He probably looked like the Hulk washing dishes.

To push a grinding machine in place of an animal may have lent itself as a picture of strength. The Philistines were not that kind to him. They were in many ways like Samson: when given the chance, they humiliated their opponent and gave no quarter.

"But the hair on his head began to grow again after it had been shaved." Each day as he sat in prison and pressed grain into flour, his hair grew a little longer. No matter the sin, the rules of nature continue. The sign of God's favor began to return over the course of his captivity. Samson knew his hair was growing. He must have wondered if his strength was returning also. Maybe he lifted his grinding stone every day to see if it ever seemed lighter than the day before. One day, he may have tossed it against the wall like a Frisbee and knew he was no longer helpless against his captors. He began to plot a way to get back at those who had trapped him, rather than repenting and asking God for the redemption of his mistakes for God's purposes. A hardened heart is tough to change.

TANGIBLE SIGNS

God has often chosen visible signs like Samson's hair to show his presence to humans. We are tactile beings. We live by sight. This is why faith is so hard for us; it is "the evidence of things we cannot see."[99] We want something our senses can receive. God knows our need. So from the rainbow after the Flood to the bronze snake in the middle of Israel's camp to the Ark of the Covenant to His Son, Jesus, God has said through tangible things, "Here I am. Trust me." God knows blind and chained humans need concrete evidence of his unseen company.

The Passover meal is one of those physical signs of God's promises. I remember the first time a Jewish friend led me through a Seder meal. The taste of the bitter herb and salt-dipped parsley led me to my own days of loss and struggle. The sweet taste of the charoset and wine reminded me of God's provisions throughout my life. The matza's stale taste heightened my hunger for a sinless life. I received the meal's blessing as one who longed to taste the presence of God. Jesus chose this ancient meal to reveal his identity and to memorialize his death for his followers. Each taste of the bread and wine is a physical reminder of a spiritual promise to the participant. Those who put their trust in the new covenant in Christ's blood confess: "We are not alone."

We have been rescued, and we have hope our Rescuer is with us every day until his return."

John tells us that "No one has ever seen God. But his only Son, who is himself God, is near to the Father's heart; he has told us about him."[100] How do you know God's character and love, and how God would act in a given situation? The answer is through his only Son, Jesus, who is our tangible evidence of God. The phrase "he has told us about him" comes from only one word in the original text, the word transliterated as *exegete*. It means to interpret or explain a word, passage, or concept. Jesus *exegetes* the Father.

My academic mentor, Dr. Bruce Corley, told me once that the word was used in ancient Greek for the guides who took people through the different temples in a city like Corinth and who explained to the curious all that went on there. John tells us Jesus is the interpretation or explanation of God. He is our guide through the temples of life and leads us to the one, true God. We cannot see God, but we can touch, hear, see, and feel Jesus through revelation, spirit, and community. Jesus, then, is *paraclete*, the Spirit of God, and *exegete*, the explanation of God.

THE GREATER GOD

Every captor celebrates the capture of his enemy. News outlets lit up when U.S. forces found Iraq's deposed despot Saddam Hussein hiding in a spider hole. The U.S. President stepped behind his official podium to announce the enemy's capture, and we celebrated another victory on the war against terrorism. The Philistines did the same when they captured their one-man terrorist organization, Samson.

Our chronicler recalls: "Now the rulers of the Philistines assembled to offer a great sacrifice to Dagon their god and to celebrate, saying, 'Our god has delivered Samson, our enemy, into our hands.'" Dagon was one of the many gods the Philistines worshipped. Apparently, its name came from the word "fish," but others claim its origin to be from a word for "grain" or "cloud." The people worshipped Dagon to ensure the growth of their crops and the cycle of the seasons much like they did the god, Baal. In their pantheon of gods, Dagon was Baal's father and so held a high place among the Philistine gods.

The rulers of Philistia threw a celebration. They gave homage to Dagon. They believed their god delivered Samson into their hands. Cynically, we could say this is what any ruler would do for political gain. Politicians know the strength of a Higher Power in gaining support from the masses. The people believed Dagon of the Philistines defeated YHWH of Israel when their soldiers delivered Samson into their hands.

Dagon as a superior god to the Lord of Israel, however, later suffered a major credibility loss when the Philistines captured the Ark of the Covenant and stored it overnight in Dagon's temple in Ashdod.[101] The morning after its capture, the image of Dagon lay prostrate before the Ark. "Must have been an earthquake," the priests explained. They set it back up in its original position, but the next day the idol was face down, and its hands and head had been cut off and placed on the threshold of the temple. Either the Israelites had superior stealth SEALs who did a superb job of creating a hoax, or something supernatural happened in the night that showed Israel's Lord to be greater than Dagon. Dagon's armies may have won the battle for the Ark, but they lost the war for supremacy in the heavens. The people of Ashdod eventually wanted nothing to do with the Ark, and they returned it to its rightful owners.

So when the people had seen Samson led before them in chains weak and humiliated, they had sung celebratory praises to their god. "Our god has delivered our enemy into our hands, the one who laid waste our land and multiplied our slain" was their praise chorus that day. They had heard the fox-tails tale. The warrior who swung the jaw of a donkey had killed their loved ones. They were ecstatic to have the one who caused them such loss. They gave their god the credit, and they were glad to give Israel's leader their justice.

WHAT GOOD IS THERE IN THIS?

As we remember this scene of the enemy's victory, we could wonder how these depressing events could possibly prove anything but a breakdown in God's plan. But in Samson's case, as with many other chosen saviors, God allows such circumstances as part of either the natural progression of sinful choices or God's discipline to bring his chosen ones back into relationship with him. Samson's sin of pride gave him over to the Philistines. God had set up the possibility of success for his servant. Samson had chosen otherwise. His circumstances were not God's doing, yet God had not abandoned him. God was still present in his life, and if Samson had not taken his own life, this humiliating failure may have brought Samson's heart into submission to God's ways.

Samson did not have to take his life. While that action may look like the inevitable end to his choices, I am convinced he could have survived to be the leader God had set him apart to become. Broken like a wild stallion, he could have become a meek yet powerful servant of God. Blinded, he would no longer be guided by the "lust of his eyes," but could now follow the promptings of the Spirit. Like blinded Neo in the third installment of the Matrix trilogy, *Matrix Revolutions*, who defeated Agent Smith after he lost his sight and his beloved Trinity, Samson could have given his life to save more than he killed on the day he died. What would Samson's power bridled under the direction of God's Spirit have looked like? Would Israel have known peace longer than twenty years? Would Samson have died in old age like King David rather than like King Saul, who fell on his sword? Sometimes blindness to the things of the world makes it possible to see the things of the kingdom of God. Sometimes imprisonment by others can be God's tool to prepare his chosen ones for the life he planned for them. Ask Joseph, who was in prison before he was in power in Egypt. Ask Paul, who was blinded for three days so he could see God's calling on his life. Ask Chuck Colson, imprisoned for Watergate crimes, who was born again there and emerged to form Prison Fellowship to serve those who are behind bars around the world.

Too many Christians fear tough times, especially American Christians. I have seen the church alive and flourishing in Russia, Albania, Cuba, and China, and I have little sympathy for whining American Christians who claim not to be "fed" or who are not "getting what they need" from the church. American Christians too often forget that they *are* the church, and they are responsible for growth in their lives and the lives of others. The church is not an institution that exists to feed overweight, wealthy people. That concept has gotten mixed up in our consumer-driven economy, where full-service church complexes have replaced the intimacy of houses as a place for followers of Jesus to gather, and seeking personal betterment has replaced building each other up when people gather as the *ekklesia*. I am thankful that trend is reversing in the small group movements around the globe.

The church is a people who follow the example of the first followers, "who . . . were of one heart and mind, and they felt that what they owned was not their own; they shared everything they had. . . . There was no poverty among them, because people who owned land or houses sold them and brought the money to the apostles to give to others in need."[102] Hard times, harassing governments, and disasters strengthen the faith of Christians around the world. Those hard aspects of life are platforms for serving others in the name of Jesus.

In America, we seem to think trouble among God's people means there is sin in our leaders' lives or God has removed his Spirit from us. When other ministries grow in number we run to them to get some of the anointing. Evangelicals often scoff at Roman Catholic and Muslim pilgrimages to holy places, yet we make the same trips to see the latest saint or shrine that can lead us closer to God. We have turned away from Jesus to preachers to exegete God for us. In our personality-driven faith, we want to see the one whose book we read or the one we saw work miracles on television. We want some of the taped experiences we see from the comfort of our home before we load up the family and head off to hear our local personality. We have forgotten that those who proclaim the message of Christ are servants, not rock stars; *we* are the church, not some credentialed professional leader. We have forgotten we follow Jesus, not the leader of a local institution or traveling road show.

When things don't go the way we want them to go in our church homes, we sense that God is "calling us to look around for another church." Too often, our readiness to abandon our congregations undermines our spiritual communities. If my sister isn't being what I think I need my sister to be, I don't casually put her aside and look for a new sister. True followers of Jesus know once they have been adopted into the family through the work of Jesus, they are always in the family. In countries where Christians are persecuted and killed and so must live in secret like followers of Christ did in the early centuries of the church, being part of the family of God is how you survive from day to day. In America, Christians treat church like they do fast food restaurants: "As long as it satisfies, I'll keep coming through the drive-through. Change the menu, and I'm off to another place of business."

Jesus warned of these attitudes. Luke tells us:

> Once, having been asked by the Pharisees when the kingdom of God would come, Jesus replied, "The kingdom of God does not come with your careful observation, nor will people say, 'Here it is,' or 'There it is,' because the kingdom of God is within you."[103]

We have forgotten that "the kingdom of God is within [us]." The kingdom is not in any ministry, denomination, or political movement. God works through people he has rescued from the dominion of darkness. Jesus' people are not a club or organization of like-minded people offering services to club members *a la* Reggie McNeal in *The Present Future*. The kingdom of God is present in the world through Christ followers who live out Jesus' teachings and Spirit in everything they do. They gather together for fellowship, worship, shared resources, and encouragement so they can stay true to their calling when they are away from the group.

Scripture tells us that hard times or God's refusal to remove pain from our lives could be part of God's discipline for his people. C. S. Lewis said that pain is God's megaphone to get our attention.[104] The writer to the Hebrews reminded his readers to "endure hardship as discipline," because "it produces a harvest of righteousness and peace for those who have been trained by it."[105] Hard times and the pain of failure are God's exercises to strengthen our muscles of faith. Just as my father disciplined me because he loved me enough to not allow me to be a spoiled brat, so God does not leave me in my arrogance to destroy myself and bring frustration to others. God either allows or orchestrates pain to guide us, change us, or deepen our relationship with him. Hebrews explains, "although he [Jesus] was a son, he learned obedience from what he suffered."[106] If suffering was the gymnasium where Christ learned obedience, we, his followers, should gladly accept the strength gained from hard times.

Samson suffered what he had coming. God was where God had always been during Samson's self-satisfying run at life—seeking to empower him to do what he was created to do. How Samson responded to the consequences of his choosing is one more difference between him and Jesus.

One Last Prayer

The Philistines' party spirit grew throughout the day. The wine flowed, and people wanted to see Dagon's prey. Like modern churchgoers, authentic worship had become boring, so they wanted entertainment added to the liturgy. I can almost hear them chanting like Duke University students at a home basketball game: "We want Samson. We want Samson." Being crowd-pleasing leaders, the rulers sent for Samson in prison. They paraded him into the center of the arena, and he began to perform feats of strength for them.

Jesus never performed for his captors. When Pilate sent his prisoner off to Herod, the Galilean tetrarch hoped the Israelite miracle worker would perform some new trick for him.[107] Jesus, however, stood silent before the earthly despot. He refused to playact a miracle worker. Charlatans and television evangelists use so-called miracles to increase revenues. Miracles, however, did not make Jesus the Son of God or increase his Nielsen Ratings. Those acts were evidence that he was who he said he was, the Creator. Jesus' miracles were the Creator returning a broken creation back to its intended form. Leprosy, lame limbs, and death were not parts of God's original creation. Jesus performed restorative acts to show God's intention for salvation in the physical as well as spiritual realm. John called Jesus' acts "signs" that pointed people to God. Jesus did not have to perform for anyone. *Being* trumps *doing* in the card game of truth.

Samson, on the other hand, obliged his captors. His acts of strength *were* who he *was*. He counted on events of brute strength to show his worth. He mustered what will he had left to show the people how strong he really was. He loved the limelight. He was Steve Nash of the Phoenix Suns in the last seconds of Game 6 of the Suns-Mavericks 2005 Western Conference semifinal showdown—a three-pointer at the buzzer to send the game into overtime. The spotlights shown on Samson again, and he was a hit. The temple was packed. Dignitaries and commoners alike had gathered for the event. Our storyteller notes that the overflow crowd on the roof numbered three thousand.

As the people shouted and watched, Samson asked the slave who was his eyes that day to show him to the main pillars so he could lean against them. The slave obliged, and Samson prepared to take his life. But first, he prayed.

This is the second of only two prayers Samson's biographer records. The first, you remember, was for water after he had worked all day to kill a thousand Philistines with the jaw of a donkey. Samson prayed when he had a need or wanted something from God. Standing between two pillars and before thousands of hecklers he prayed, "O Sovereign LORD, remember me. O God, please strengthen me just once more."

He prayed that God would remember him, but Samson had forgotten God, not the other way around. God had been by his side from his birth through his captivity. Samson also cried out for God to give him savior-like strength. How wonderful this appears! The man surely had been broken by his capture and imprisonment. He had repented of his selfishness. He was a new man, and he begged for his strength back in order to serve God. We want to believe this is true. What a great sermon illustration this would make! But then, we hear the next part of his plea: "and let me with one blow get revenge on the Philistines for my two eyes." Never mind. Scratch the scene where Samson's heart is changed. Our hero is still the guy we have watched all along. Samson wanted his strength to get personal revenge on the people who gouged his eyes out. He had no intention of changing his interests to serve others. His death, like his life, would serve his needs above others'.

How different Samson's prayer was than that of Jesus on the night before his death. Jesus, who would allow his capture in order to complete the Plan, bowed in prayer to God, saying, "My Father, if it is possible, may this cup be taken from me. Yet not as I will, but as you will"[108] Yes, Jesus wanted another way to fulfill the purpose of his life other than death on a cross. He had seen too many die of exposure and brutality as they hung on the roadside going into Jerusalem. The Romans flaunted their death machines in order to keep the masses in check. Jesus knew what it meant to go to the cross. His humanity tried to convince him to do almost anything other than be tortured and treated like an animal to pay the price for the sins of the world. Satan's offers were as tempting that night as they were at the beginning of his ministry, but Jesus' heart was captured by the will of the Father, not his desire to avoid pain. Rather than praying for strength to avenge the hurts people would inflict on him, he prayed to God, *Yet not as I will, but as you will.* Jesus submitted not to his fears, but to the will of his Father.

Later, on the cross, Jesus prayed, "Father, forgive them; for they do not know what they are doing."[109] Just as he had washed the feet of the one who betrayed him, he prayed forgiveness for those who nailed him to the cross. As Max Lucado titled his book, *No Wonder They Call Him the Savior.* Only the Son of God could act that way toward those who sought to kill him. Samson was incapable of such a prayer. His heart never submitted to God's purposes. The prayers of our two saviors at their deaths demonstrate the depth of their differences as leaders of God's people.

DEATH

This is how Samson's life ended:

> Then Samson reached toward the two central pillars on which the temple stood. Bracing himself against them, his right hand on the one and his left hand on the other, Samson said, "Let me die with the Philistines!" Then he pushed with all his might, and down came the temple on the rulers and all the people in it.

Samson's life story ended with one last shout to die with his enemies and a tremendous act of strength. He could no longer see to maim. He was in chains and could no longer attack at will. So he brought down the temple on himself with all who gathered to gawk at his weakness. A warrior's sacrifice dealt a wounding blow to the enemy. Although a suicide, Samson's death scored a win for our side.

Note that with Samson's prayer and cry to die with his enemies, we do not read that "the Spirit of the Lord came upon him in power." The Spirit of the Lord had left him when Delilah oversaw the cutting of his hair. His hair and strength returned, but we are not told the Spirit of the Lord visited him again. This was Samson's doing. The flame of the Lord's Spirit watched from the sidelines. With his own strength he brought on his own death and the death of his enemies; the temple collapsed as he pushed with all his might.

King Saul of Israel's reign ended in much the same way. God chose the handsome son of Kish at the people's insistence to become Israel's first king. When he arrived at Gibeah, the home of prophets, Samuel tells us "the Spirit of God came upon him in power."[110] Like Samson, Saul received power from the Spirit of God to complete God's mission for his life. Yet, the king-messenger would step away from the flame of the Spirit's presence when he did not carry out God's instructions against the Amalekites. Samuel summed up why God removed his favor from his king:

To obey is better than sacrifice,
And to heed is better than the fat of rams.
For rebellion is like the sin of divination,
And arrogance like the evil of idolatry.
Because you have rejected the word of the LORD,
He has rejected you as king.[111]

From that day on, Saul was left to rule in his own strength while his successor, David, waited in the desert to take the throne. The flame of God's influence in Saul's life flickered and stopped burning at his choice to keep King Agag as a spoil of war instead of following God's command to destroy everything and to take nothing. King Saul ended his life like Samson. When he saw his inevitable defeat, he fell on his sword. Many Philistines died at his hand during his reign, but the last life he took was his own.

Samson allowed his lover to cut his braids. Saul allowed his men to keep some spoils of war. Both acts of disobedience brought the loss of God's power in their lives. Both heroes committed suicide after their lives had spun off anything worthy to be salvaged.

Suicide is the ultimate act of selfishness. Left alone to solve their problems or heal their pain, these men took their lives because they believed they were the only ones who could bring an end to the suffering. Theirs were desperate acts in order to overcome despair. Paul's proverb is true, "Godly sorrow brings repentance that leads to salvation and leaves no regret, but worldly sorrow brings death."[112] King Saul and Samson did not allow their sorrow to lead to salvation. The sorrow brought on by their doing brought death. Their lives did not end in victory—yes, enemies lay dead with them on the battlefield, but their lives ended as wasted possibilities.

Jesus never disobeyed his Father in heaven. The writer to the Hebrews reminds us this High Priest of ours understands our weaknesses, for he faced all of the same temptations we do, yet he did not sin.[113] The difference between Samson, Saul, and Jesus was that the true Savior never crossed the line of disobedience. He never lost the flame of God's Spirit because he never walked outside the path marked for him by the Father. He did not fall on his sword or bring down a roof on his head. Jesus climbed on the cross out of obedience to his Father's Plan for his life. A willing sacrifice bought us our right standing before Holy God.

The Value of a Death

Our storyteller measured Samson's death by writing, "Thus he killed many more when he died than while he lived." Heroes become legends when their lives end in spectacular acts for their country. Samson died a hero. He soon became a legend. The flame that accompanied his life, however, was extinguished, and the messenger of God was laid to rest. His life was over.

Jesus' death was as different from Samson's as was his capture and prayer the night before he died. Jesus did not die to avenge his enemies but to forgive them. Jesus could have called upon legions of angels to kill more than three thousand, but he chose to complete God's calling on his life. Jesus' cry on the cross before he died was, "It is finished." Jesus' death on the cross was his mission. He completed it.

Jesus' death was about the redemption of the world, not the destruction of his earthly enemies. Samson destroyed the temple of Dagon. It would need to be rebuilt before worshippers could gather again to offer sacrifice to a lifeless god. At Jesus' death, the curtain that separated the Holy of Holies from the rest of the world was torn from top to bottom. Access to God became available to everyone through Jesus. Now no temple is needed other than the body of the faithful to house the presence of God. The final High Priest offered himself as the final sacrifice, which bought salvation for all peoples. No more Samson-like deaths were necessary to bring life to God's people.

Those affected by Jesus' death far surpassed the number touched by Samson's cave-in of Dagon's temple. Like principal that continues to give dividends after its investment, Jesus' death affects people's lives even today. Samson's heroic death that killed some of Israel's enemies served its purpose at a point in history. Jesus' humble death in history served its eternal purpose to give life to God's enemies, all of whom have fallen short of God's expectations of righteousness.

Samson's death brought a temporary reprieve from Israel's enemies. Jesus' death brought a permanent pardon from God's wrath to those who claim his work on the cross as their righteousness. Samson's death dealt a blow to the Philistines, Israel's enemy. Jesus' death killed the enemy of all, death.

BURIAL

"Then his brothers and his father's whole family went down to get him. They brought him back and buried him between Zorah and Eshtaol in the tomb of Manoah his father." Samson's family fulfilled their obligation to retrieve their relative's body and to bury him in the tomb of his father. It was a proper burial for one of Israel's sons. No friends seem to have joined in mourning his death. You would think the tribes of Israel would send representatives to show their respect for the one who kept their enemies out of their fields for twenty years, but to all appearances, no one was compelled to honor the fallen hero. The hometown hero did not get a parade the day he came home in a casket. His family quietly carried him to his father's resting place. There he lies until the resurrection of the dead.

Only Jesus' mother, Mary Magdalene, and the disciple whom he loved remained at the cross on the day of his death. His family—most of whom thought he was crazy—probably did not show their faces. Like Samson, Jesus' earthly father, Joseph, was no longer on the scene. He most likely had died before he saw the death of his son. These were the only four who braved the ridicule and possible retribution by the religious authorities to stand at the cross. Jesus, like his Old Testament counterpart, did not have a fanfare as he was carried from the cross to the donated tomb of Joseph of Arimathaea. But unlike Samson, the grave was not Jesus' final resting place. The tomb became ground zero of a new creation. The Creator was the firstborn of his new created order.

Jesus' friends and followers buried him, but the flame that engulfed his life did not go out. The Messenger of God was raised on the third day and became the hope for eternity. Forty days later, he ascended into heaven to take his place in the Godhead. What happened to the flame of his Spirit? At the Jewish festival called Pentecost, some fifty days after Jesus' death, the flame of Jesus' power in what "seemed to be tongues of fire came to rest on each of them."[114] Those 120 followers who gathered for prayer became bathed in the flame of God's Spirit. They became messengers of the Good News of Jesus cloaked in the fire of the Holy Spirit.

This Pentecost flame is no longer limited to God's heroes—a chosen one or two with unique missions like Samson. It is available to everyone who calls Jesus Rescuer and Leader. The Spirit of the Lord does not show up just for heroic feats. It dwells in each follower to produce the fruit of the Spirit[115] and to empower his adopted children for acts of power and love. We are the ambassadors of Christ, who walk in the flame of God's Spirit through a relationship with God's Son.

We don't need the strength and beauty of Samson to do the will of God. We don't need to perform heroic deeds to make it into the list of the faithful.

We don't need an extraordinary experience to be engulfed by God's presence. All we need is to trust the Savior who ransomed us from sin and enshrouds us with his Spirit.

STILL A HERO

Samson did not live the complete life God had planned for him. He married a foreign woman, slept with prostitutes, and sold out the secret of his God-given strength to a seductress, yet he finds his place in what some call the Hall of Faith; those portraits that hang in the family room near the backdoor of your spiritual ancestors' homes.

> Well, how much more do I need to say? It would take too long to recount the stories of the faith of Gideon, Barak, Samson, Jephthah, David, Samuel, and all the prophets. By faith these people overthrew kingdoms, ruled with justice, and received what God had promised them. They shut the mouths of lions, quenched the flames of fire, and escaped death by the edge of the sword. Their weakness was turned to strength. They became strong in battle and put whole armies to flight.[116]

Looking back, the writer to the Hebrews saw in Samson someone worthy to be honored as one of the faithful. What did he see? Samson did not "overthrow a kingdom." He didn't "rule with justice," and he didn't "receive what God had promised him." That's for sure. He squandered God's promise. He did "shut the mouth" of *one* lion, but David did that more times than Samson. Samson "quenched the flame" of God's fire in his life, but that is not what the writer is talking about here. Samson did "escape death by a sword," but he died as if he had fallen on his own sword. Samson's greatest weaknesses did not turn to strengths. That leaves "they became strong in battle and put whole armies to flight" as Samson's epitaph.

Samson became strong in battle through the Spirit of the LORD and the Philistines scattered in defeat. This savior has his place in faith's history because he was an instrument of God's protection of Israel. Those inspired to look back through the pages of His-story saw Samson as one of those whom God had chosen to serve his purposes. He made the list in the New Testament, and that's something. I want my name in the list when I enter eternity.

Merrill Tenney likened the New Testament to the Old like fruit to the roots of the tree. Without the roots, the fruit would never come, and without fruit, the roots never complete their purpose. Samson was part of the root system that produced the fruit of the Messiah. He belongs in the New Testament list as one of our spiritual ancestors who failed to live out God's purposes in his life completely but who God used to point us to our final Rescuer, Jesus. God used the selfish use of Samson's gifts and his unchecked appetites to accomplish God's will, but God's grace and sovereignty is no license to live like Samson. Our example of a God-purposed life is Jesus, the one who lived in the flame of the Father's presence and who completed his mission as assigned.

The writer to the Hebrews encouraged his readers to trust God even when they could not see physical evidence of God's Plan. This is why God inspired him to make the record of faithful followers. Not fully seeing God's Plan in our lifetime may appear as if God has abandoned us or his promises are empty, but the faithful find strength in trusting God and being obedient to what God has called us to do. So many have gone before us who did not see what they trusted God to give them; then suddenly in the midst of their struggles to be obedient to God's call they got a glimpse of his promise to them. God's use of our crazy uncles and royal aunts of faith give us hope that God can use our feeble efforts to accomplish some part of his plan for all people.

Success

One more word about the success of each savior before we leave them: if you were to evaluate their lives by the number of people each man touched, you might conclude that Samson was the more successful of the two. After all, he murdered more people, thereby causing wide-spreading ripple effects of grief and economic instability among his people's enemies. A ridiculous idea, huh?

But how many times do we judge the success of a person's life by arbitrary standards without considering the validity of our criteria? How many times do we rank ministries and ministers by the count connected to what they do? How many times have you thought small equals less blessing and large means more? Ronald Heifetz and Marty Linsky remind us in *Leadership on the Line* that you can't measure meaning and that "if you save one life, you save the world."[117] The measure of success in the kingdom is faithfulness to God's calling on your life.

Faithfulness, however, does not guarantee you will realize all your dreams. I have learned this in almost forty years of trying to be faithful to God's call on my life. When I began as a pastor, I saw a small band of believers meeting in a showroom space growing into a megachurch. That sort of thing was happening in Chicago, Orange County, and Dallas. "Why couldn't it happen with my ministry?" I thought. Collin County was the second-fastest growing county in America at the time. All the factors were in place.

The wild card in my ministry was the call to reach those who either had no place for church in their lives or who had been wounded by it in some way. That call meant we would gather Christ followers who wanted to invest their lives in service to others. This meant change, which in "the evangelical capital of the world" is not necessary for those who seek name-brand religion and minimal church-going obligations. Morphing into a fresh expression of the church in a conventional town where Christians are saturated with weekend options of faith is difficult. Don't get me wrong. I take responsibility for every operational or decision-making misstep along the journey of transitioning to become a mission outpost in our mission field, but I know personally that simply because you say yes to Jesus when he walks by your boat and calls you to follow him, you don't necessarily end up successful in worldly terms. You will "drink the cup" and "you will be baptized with [his] baptism" before it is all over.[118]

Faithfulness, however, does ensure you will get a glimpse of God's vision for your life. A myth among Christians is that if we follow all the rules and do what the preacher tells us to do we will be blessed, which in today's America too often means to have SUVs, excellent health, and trips to Disney World. The only problem with that conclusion is that Jesus said his kingdom is "not of this world."[119] Our hoping for earthly things as a blessing from God is like fish long-ing to sit in lounge chairs on the beach they swim by every day.

My ministry has been nothing like what I dreamed it would be when I was in seminary, but I would not change a day—okay, maybe a day or two—of what I have experienced as I have tried to be faithful to God's call on my life and church. I have had a peek at God's vision for his church on earth. I have seen firsthand what a group of people called out to be a unique expression of the body of Christ is like. I have had a glimpse around the corner of how God is reviving and reforming the church in this part of the world. Radically changed lives, powerful expressions of love, and an authentically healthy group of Christ followers are the blessings God has allowed me to see. I would not exchange seeing those things for my measly dreams, nor would I trade this adventure for the career path I thought I was to follow.

Faithfulness, not success, is the measure of those called to join God in the redemptive dance of history.

Why is this so? Our True Savior modeled the blessed life for us. He was faithful to the Father's call on his life, and his life ended on the cross, the goal of his mission. Yet it was in his faithfulness to the cross that he was raised to a new creation that ultimately would outlive the first world he formed. Those who follow Jesus long to hear one thing in eternity: "Well done, good and faithful servant."[120] The earthly results of their faithfulness does not factor into the eter-nal equation. They simply desire to bring the talents of the Master they have doubled to the One who trusted them with his property in the first place.

To follow Jesus is to become a faithful angel in the flame: a messenger with the truth of love and hope through Jesus, faithful to the One who gave us that message, engulfed with his Spirit. Your journey may not fulfill your dreams, but you can rest at night knowing God will use you in some way to complete his cosmic plan to capture the hearts of men and women with the love of God.

Discussion Questions _____

1. What historic deaths would you classify as ill-timed or tragic? What deaths have you known to be purposeful or heroic?

2. Although Jesus and Samson appeared to be captured enemies of the state, how were their circumstances different according to the author?

3. How does the explanation of Jesus as the "exegete of God" aid your understanding of who he is?

4. What have you experienced that seemed to have been a failure on God's part but later revealed to be exactly what needed to happen?

5. How have hard times served to reveal God's character and purposes to you and shaped your character?

6. How were Jesus' and Samson's last prayers and deaths similar? How were they different? How did Jesus' prayer and death reveal who he was?

7. Do you agree or disagree with the author's description of success in the things of God? What evidence of this explanation have you seen in your life? If you disagree, why?

Epilogue

I hope that by meeting Jesus through the backdoor of his ancestor Samson has helped you grow in your faith in God. I pray you now know a bit more about your spiritual heritage. I pray you can begin to see yourself as an angel in the flame of God's Presence as you follow Jesus. I long for you to know the blessings of God's vision for your life.

God has chosen you, like he chose Samson, to be a savior for your family and church against their enemies. Your calling is irrevocable. Your choices are redeemable. Go boldly into life trusting these things are true.

You have a choice to make as you return to the stuff of life. You can live as Samson, for yourself, and maybe experience a few intrusions of God's Spirit into your life from time to time, or you can live for Jesus, as a servant of God, one of his messengers, and find your greatest joy in knowing you are offering, every day, all that you are and have back to God as an act of worship.

You are welcome to return to your ancestors' houses through the backdoor any time you want to hear more stories about them and their exploits. Guests and family alike have a place at the table. Pull up a chair and get out the family album of Scripture. Let the stories begin.

Endnotes

[1] Deuteronomy 6:11

[2] Judges 2:11

[3] Judges 2:18 NKJV

[4] Hebrews 13:2

[5] Genesis 6:4; Numbers 13:33

[6] Isaiah 6:2

[7] Genesis 18

[8] Daniel 10:4-11

[9] Luke 1:19

[10] Luke 1:30

[11] Judges 13:5

[12] Luke 1:33

[13] Hebrews 11:6 MSG

[14] Exodus 20:7

[15] Philippians 2:10, 11

[16] Numbers 6:10, 11

[17] Mark 10:38

[18] See 1 Peter 1:12.

[19] Psalm 139:6

[20] 2 Kings 2:11

[21] 1 Thessalonians 2:7, for example.

[22] 1 Corinthians 6:19

[23] Romans 12:1, 2

[24] 2 Corinthians 3:18 MSG

[25] Acts 6:15 NLT

[26] Ephesians 5:2

[27] John 4:24

[28] Acts 2:1–3

[29] Isaiah 6:5

[30] Exodus 33:20

[31] John 1:45, 46

[32] Innovative Church Conference, July 1999, Glorieta Conference Center, New Mexico.

[33] 1 John 2:16

[34] Matthew 6:22

[35] Joshua 23:12, 13

[36] Rick Warren, *The Purpose Driven Life* (Grand Rapids: Zondervan, 2002), 65-66.

[37] 1 Corinthians 10:31

[38] Donald Miller, *Blue Like Jazz* (Nashville: Thomas Nelson, 2003), 182.

[39] Romans 8:28

[40] Anne Lamott, *Traveling Mercies* (Anchor Books, 1999), 61.

[41] Luke 13:10–13

[42] John 6:38

[43] John 15:13

[44] Proverbs 17:17

[45] John 10:11

[46] Psalm 55:12–14

[47] 1 Chronicles 27:33

[48] 2 Samuel 15:31

[49] John 19:26

[50] Proverbs 16:18

[51] Luke 7:41, 42

[52] Luke 15

[53] Matthew 13

[54] Matthew 13:34, 35; Psalm 78:2

[55] Matthew 5:3, 5

[56] Matthew 19:5; my paraphrase

[57] Deuteronomy 19:21

[58] Judges 3:10

[59] Judges 6:34

[60] Judges 11:29

[61] Matthew 3:16

[62] Judges 15:4, 5

[63] Matthew 5:38–42

[64] Matthew 26:67, 68

[65] Judges 15:14

[66] Proverbs 13:10

[67] Proverbs 20:18

[68] Matthew 14:23

[69] Judges 5

[70] Psalm 144:9, 10

[71] Psalm 108:12, 13

[72] Psalm 35:1, 2

[73] Psalm 33:16–19

[74] Ephesians 6:19, 20

[75] 2 Corinthians 12:9, 10

[76] Luke 5:16

[77] Proverbs 5:8–14

[78] Deuteronomy 23:17, 18

[79] Leviticus 21:7

[80] Judges 17:6

[81] 1 John 2:16

[82] Frederic Buechner, *Wishful Thinking: A Seeker's ABC* (San Francisco: Harper & Row, 1973), 54.

[83] James 1:13

[84] Hebrews 4:15

[85] Mark 10:45

[86] 1 Corinthians 7:3–5

[87] 1 Corinthians 15:32

[88] Proverbs 11:7

[89] John Eldredge, *Epic: The Story God Is Telling and the Role that Is Yours to Play* (Nashville: Thomas Nelson, 2004), 15.

[90] Luke 4:18, 19; Isaiah 61:1, 2

[91] Luke 19:10

[92] Mark 10:44, 45

[93] Luke 23:3

[94] Matthew 5:14–16

[95] 2 Corinthians 3:1–3

[96] Mark 5:30

[97] John 15:11, 18

[98] See http://www.studylight.org/enc/isb/view.cgi?number=T6048

[99] Hebrews 11:1 NLT

[100] John 1:18 NLT

[101] 1 Samuel 5:1–7

[102] Acts 4:32–35

[103] Luke 17:20–21

[104] Quoted in C. S. Lewis, *The Joyful Christian* (New York: Macmillan, 1977), 210.

[105] Hebrews 12:4–11

[106] Hebrews 5:8

[107] Luke 23:8

[108] Matthew 26:39

[109] Luke 23:34

[110] 1 Samuel 10:10

[111] 1 Samuel 15:22, 23

[112] 2 Corinthians 7:10

[113] Hebrews 4:15

[114] Acts 2:3

[115] Galatians 5:22, 23

[116] Hebrews 11:32–34

[117] Ronald Heifetz and Marty Linsky, *Leadership on the Line* (Cambridge: Harvard Business School Press, 2002), 212.

[118] Mark 10:39

[119] John 18:36

[120] Matthew 25:23